LUTHER & HIS WORLD

GRAHAM TOMLIN

Published by Lion Books
an imprint of
Lion Hudson plc
Wilkinson House, Jordan Hill Road,
Oxford OX2 8DR, England
www.lionhudson.com/lion
ISBN 978 0 7459 5588 9
e-ISBN 978 0 7459 5707 4

First edition 2002
This edition 2012

Acknowledgments
Scripture quotations are from *The Revised
Standard Version of the Bible* copyright © 1346,
1952 and 1971 by the Division of Christian
Education of the National Council of
Churches in the USA. Used by permission.

A catalogue record for this book is available
from the British Library

Printed and bound in Malta, July 2012, LH28

Contents

Introduction

By any account, Martin Luther must rank as one of the most influential European figures of the last millennium. Marco Polo and Columbus opened up new continents, Shakespeare and Michelangelo produced some of the most sublime pieces of art, and Napoleon and Hitler changed the political face of their centuries. Yet Luther and the Reformation he triggered have made a huge impact not just on Europe, but also on North America, Australia and – by means of the Protestant missionary movement – throughout the rest of the world. Protestantism shaped a whole new way of life for countless people across the Western world and beyond, which coloured their approaches to God, work, politics, leisure, family – in fact, almost every aspect of human life. It played a seminal role in the early development and continuing self-image of the United States, and in the emergence of democracy and economic and religious freedoms in Europe.

> 'To people of all nationalities the first Protestants bequeathed in spite of themselves a heritage of spiritual freedom and equality, the consequences of which are still working themselves out in the world today.'
>
> **Stephen Ozment,** *Protestants*, 1992

Protestantism was one of the key movements ushering in changes from the medieval to the modern world. Luther cannot claim credit nor can he be blamed for the whole of what eventually became Protestantism, but as one who played a critical role in the emergence of a new church and a new way of life for millions of people, the influence of his actions and beliefs on the past 500 years has been incalculable. The modern world can barely be understood without them.

Yet who was Luther? During the 500 years since he lived, Martin Luther has been seen as just about everything: from an infallible teacher of the truth (17th-century Lutheran orthodoxy), to the supreme example of rationalist individualism (the Enlightenment), to the man chiefly responsible for the German churches' near total failure to oppose the rise of the Nazis in 1930s Germany. Alongside this, the Roman Catholic judgment has changed from seeing Luther as the arch-heretic who fatally split a united European Christendom, to a much more sympathetic understanding, almost claiming him as one of their own in recent years.

This book, naturally, paints its own portrait of Luther. It paints a picture of a man struggling with some of the deepest of all human questions – if there is a God, is he good? Can he be trusted? What or who is the power that lies behind the universe? Luther battled with these questions in a profound and sometimes agonizing way from very early in his life. He tried the various contemporary solutions on offer, including the monastic and the academic life, before stumbling upon an answer which stilled his fears and satisfied the deepest yearnings of his soul. In the process, the church in Europe, already going through a period of great upheaval, experienced dramatic change and deep division. Luther was one part of a large and complex story, but he remains a key figure in the development of the modern world. In recent years, the emphasis among historians has been to view the Reformation as an economic or sociological phenomenon, and to concentrate not so much on the 'big names' of the movement, but rather on exploring how it affected ordinary people in Germany, Switzerland and beyond. These approaches have yielded some invaluable results and have helped people to understand the movement far better than ever before. Nonetheless, the Reformation was still, however, a movement sparked off by particular people writing particular ideas, which then had an effect far wider and greater than they could have envisaged. And Luther, as perhaps the chief of these people, deserves study even now.

This book tries to present an accessible and attractive modern introduction to Luther's life, ideas and significance for today, in which recent scholarly research on Luther is implicit but not intrusive. The author's hope is that it will stimulate readers to read Luther for themselves. Many medieval and Renaissance writers are pretty turgid and tedious to read. Luther is neither of these things. A facility with language, a colourful imagination and a blunt Saxon frankness all combine to make his writing hold attention, even when tackling obscure aspects of late-medieval theology. Luther is rarely dull. At the end of this book, a list of suggestions for further reading points the way for those who want to explore his significance a little further.

CHAPTER 1

The Friar

Eisleben was a mining town. Even today the surrounding landscape is punctuated with dark conical slag heaps, the unmistakable scars of excavation. It was never the prettiest of places, but it was at least prosperous, and as the 15th century drew towards its close, it was already attracting many expectant prospectors from further afield in Thuringia and beyond. Among the hopeful new arrivals was Hans Luder. He had come from the village of Möhra but, as his younger brother had inherited the family farmland on his father's death, according to the local custom on inheritance, Hans had to find some other way of making a living. Having worked in the mines of Möhra for a few years, he wanted to move into mine management or ownership. Eisleben seemed a good bet, being a thriving centre of copper extraction. So, in the early summer of 1483, he moved to the town with his pregnant wife, Margarethe, renting lodgings whilst he tried his luck in the business of mining.

Margarethe Luder finally produced her second child on 10 November that year. A day later, the baby boy was taken to St Peter's and St Paul's, the nearest church, just a few yards away from the house, where he was duly baptized. He was given the name of the saint whose day it was: Martin. Eisleben did not prove a successful venture for Hans Luder. Competition was fierce, and he was only one among many trying to forge a living out of copper. Within another year, he had moved on, this time to Mansfeld. Here, he managed to borrow money from some wealthy merchants. He leased a smelting works from the counts of Mansfeld, and gained part ownership in a number of mines. Even though it took him many years to pay off his loans – and meanwhile the family had to live frugally and carefully – Hans was upwardly mobile, ambitious and determined.

Margarethe Luder had eight or nine children, of whom three or four died young – no one could quite remember how many, because infant mortality was such a common part of life. Martin, the eldest of the surviving children, was clearly bright. He was especially close to his brother, Jacob, and endured what was a strict, but not unusual, upbringing. His father's ambition stretched not just to his business concerns, but also to his son's education, especially as he showed some academic potential during his early years at the school in Mansfeld. Rather than take the usual course of training Martin to inherit the family business, Hans Luder decided to make whatever sacrifices were necessary to ensure a good education for his son.

In Mansfeld itself, educational possibilities were limited, so when he was 13, Martin was sent 40 miles down the River Elbe to a school in Magdeburg, a much bigger town of 12,000 inhabitants. Here, the young scholar encountered the life of a large city for the first time. For some unknown reason, Hans then moved Martin on to Eisenach. He perhaps hoped, vainly as it turned out, that some of his relations there would take the boy in. He did, however, find lodgings with the affluent Cotta and Schalbe families, who were noted for their simple generosity and genuine piety, which contrasted with the strict regime and strenuous social aspirations of his own home. Martin always spoke with great fondness of Eisenach as *meine liebe Stadt* – 'my dear town'.

School, like Martin's father, was strict. Martin once recalled being soundly beaten for failing to conjugate a verb which he had not yet learned. In Mansfeld, and then in Eisenach, under his teacher Wiegand Güldennapf, he became word perfect in Latin and German grammar. He learned the basics of the church's

'I was born in Eisleben, and baptized in St Peter's there. I do not remember this, but I believe my parents and fellow countrymen.'

Martin Luther in a letter to Georg Spalatin, January 1520

liturgy, singing for extra income as a choirboy in St George's, the main parish church in the centre of the town, as well as from house to house. Luder's ambitions for his promising son did not end in Eisenach, however. He clearly wanted him to enter a less precarious and more prestigious trade than his own, so in 1501 he decided that Martin should gain a good university education and prepare for a life as a lawyer.

University days

The city of Erfurt was bigger than anything that Martin had yet seen, and its famous university was already nearly 150 years old. The university itself lay tucked into a bend in the River Gera, which meandered through the crowded city. Erfurt boasted about 36 different churches, their spires straining into the sky. It was home to at least 11 houses of different religious monastic orders. As a result, Erfurt was known in Germany as 'little Rome'. It was, by the standards of the time, a significant place, and the size of its great cathedral, as well as the numerous churches, must have made quite an impression on any young student arriving for the first time. By the time Martin arrived there, the university was, to a certain extent, living on its past reputation. He later commented on how the most popular 'courses' were those offered in the inns and taverns of the city, referring to the university as 'a bawdy house and a beer house'.

Nevertheless, this was an exciting venture for this 17-year-old, as for the first time he entered the university setting in which he was to spend most of his life. In Erfurt, as in all European universities of the time, the Greek philosopher Aristotle was the chief authority. His ideas were used as a basic guide to examining important questions in all subjects. Like all students in the Faculty of Arts, Martin first studied logic, dialectics, rhetoric and grammar – in other words, the methods he would have to use in his future education – all through the lens of Aristotle. In the second year, students would progress to study Aristotle's texts on ethics, politics, economics and metaphysics, the study of abstract ideas and realities, beyond [meta-] physics. From there, they would move on to music, mathematics, geometry and astronomy. By this stage, having received the status of 'Master', Martin should have received a good general training in all the liberal arts, from which he could move on to specialize in a chosen field, such as Theology, Law or Medicine.

Students at the university lived in special lodgings or *bursa*. For most of his time, Martin Luder (he later changed his name to the more sophisticated-sounding Luther) probably stayed in a hostel called St George's, on the banks of the small, gently flowing river, just to the north of the university area. Here, life was strictly supervised. The day began and ended in chapel, and meals were eaten to the accompaniment of readings from the Bible, or other suitable books. Students slept together, crammed into small dormitories, and the warden kept a close eye on his lodgers – even having a say in their final results.

Martin's early university career was nothing special. He came an undistinguished 30th out of 57 in his baccalaureate examinations at the end of his first year, perhaps as a result of his slow educational start in Mansfeld. Gradually, however, his ability began to emerge. Although 300 had started with him, Luther was one of only 17 students who finally graduated as Master of Arts in February 1505, being placed second in his year.

From that point, the plan was to specialize in law. Hans Luder's natural hope was that Martin would progress towards a respectable career in a legal, civic or even political position as an advisor to the local sovereign, the Elector. Yet within months, that plan was ruined by a dramatic event which changed the course of his life for ever.

Luther and religion

While Martin Luther was in many respects an ordinary, if gifted, student – sociable, musical, popular and religious – in another respect, he stood apart from his peers. He seemed

to possess an unusually scrupulous nature, and suffered from bouts of depression or, as the medievals called it, Despair. Scholars have for years tried to identify the source of these episodes, which seem to have combined physical, spiritual and psychological symptoms.

Whatever personal factors were involved, Luther's anxieties were inevitably tied up with religion. Popular religion at the time was strongly tinged with a fear of death and the following judgment. Earthly life was a brief interlude of preparation for the real thing – eternity to come – which would either be spent with the saints in everlasting blessedness, or tormented by devils in an eternity of conscious pain. Which of these was your fate depended on how this life was spent. As so often in Christian history, the fear of hell was more vivid than the desire for heaven. The Christ of much late-medieval art was the fearsome judge, brooding over the world, the sword of judgment coming out of one ear, the lily of mercy out of the other, watching over the division of humanity into 'saved' and 'damned' with impassive justice. Manuals on preparing for dying, skeletal monuments on tombs in churches and, of course, images of the dying Christ on the cross helped to focus the mind of the medieval Christian on the inevitability of death and the judgment of God.

Meditations on the death and passion of Christ encouraged penitents to feel sympathy with his sufferings, and sorrow for their sins, which made him die. The questions of judgment were foremost in many minds. Would God have mercy on me? Would God be gracious, ushering me into the company of heaven? Or would he be condemning, banishing me to endless anguish, aware of what I have missed out on, an agony which can never know an end? Luther was all too aware of these questions, and felt them more keenly than most. He also knew of the one sure way of forestalling the judgment to come – to enter a monastery.

Preparing for death in the Middle Ages

Medieval people were keenly aware of the nearness of death. Many manuals appeared to help to prepare Christians for the moment of dying. Dietrich Kolde's *Mirror for Christians*, a catechism for uneducated laypeople which was published in 1470, included the following instructions:

When it gets to the point of separation, or when bitter death is coming, then you should say the following repeatedly: 'O holy God! O powerful God! O compassionate God! O strict and righteous judge, have mercy on me, a poor sinner, when I must answer at your terrifyingly strict court, and when I give testimony as a poor human being about all my words and all my deeds. O dear Jesus, then may your holy bitter death, your precious blood and your unspeakable suffering stand between you and all my sins… O Mary, let me never hear the voice of Jesus the strict judge. O gentle, compassionate and sweet Mary, stand by me now, because today I must fight a battle on which my poor soul's eternal bliss or eternal damnation depends.'

A new direction

Luther returned to Erfurt to take up his legal studies in May 1505, after a period of characteristic melancholy. It seems he was not entirely happy with his father's wishes for him. They had argued about the way ahead, but his father had the parental right to dictate what his son should do. However, unexpected events were soon to change Luther's direction in life.

Luther had already had one brush with death. Some years before, he was walking out in the fields with a friend when he slipped and fell. As he did so, the short dagger which he, like most students, carried pierced his thigh and ruptured an artery. He was in serious danger of bleeding to death, and would have done so, had his friend not been able to call for help. During the summer of 1505, he made a brief trip back home to Mansfeld. One warm day early in July, he was walking back to Erfurt, ready to resume his work the next day. Dark clouds had gathered and a summer storm began. As he passed within half a mile or so of a small village called Stotternheim, a bolt of lightning flashed into the field beside him, knocking him to the ground in terror. In a moment of naked panic, the inner instincts of his heart came suddenly to the surface, as he cried out 'Blessed St Anne! I will become a monk!' (St Anne was the patron saint of miners, his father's profession, and a popular saint of the time.)

'Afterwards, I regretted the vow, and others tried to dissuade me. But I stuck to it... I never dreamed of leaving the monastery.'

Martin Luther, 'Table Talk', January 1538

Badly shaken, Luther continued the remaining miles of his journey to Erfurt, and told his friends of what had happened. They had no inkling of his spiritual distress, and the new vow came as a complete surprise. Most advised him to ignore it; some said he should keep it. Luther himself was in no doubt that he should abide by what he had promised.

A decision by such a talented student to enter the monastery was by no means unusual – yet it was drastic. This was to exchange the relatively carefree world of a scholar for a life of severe mortification and self-denial. Luther knew exactly the kind of life he was letting himself in for, and why he was entering the monastery. This was no desire for an easy life, enjoying the fruits of the monastery field and cellar. Nor was it running away from his father. He did it to save his soul. It was an attempt, somehow, to please and appease the God of judgment, who was waiting for him at the moment of death. It was out of a simple desire to find a God who would forgive and love him that he embarked on this new, more intense quest in the spiritual rigours of monastic life.

'I took the vow not for the sake of my belly, but for the sake of my salvation, and I observed all our statutes very strictly.'

Martin Luther, 'Table Talk', March 1539

So, against his father's will and the advice of many friends, just a fortnight later, having cancelled his registration on the law course, Luther walked the few yards across the bridge from St George's Hostel, up the narrow lane leading to the door of the monastery of the Order of Augustinian Friars, knocked and asked for admittance. He became a 'postulant' for a few weeks, still wearing his old clothes, while the prior of the monastery considered his request for entry. A few weeks later, he was admitted as a 'novice'. During the ceremony, he lay prostrate before the altar in the chapel of the monastery, arms extended in the shape of a cross, to symbolize the sacrifices he was about to make. A list was read out of the hardships of life in the monastery, including the long hours reciting services in chapel, the limited diet, the subduing of the flesh, and the need to beg in the streets. After various prayers, hymns and vows, the new postulant was formally handed over to the novice master, who would supervise his progress in the probationary year, until he could be admitted as a full member of the order. His hair was shaven on top, to create the normal friar's 'tonsure', and, for the first time, Martin Luther dressed in monastic novice's garb.

When his father found out what he had done, he was furious. The years of sacrifice he had made to give his son a good education, his plans to see his gifted eldest son marry and settle down into a good and lucrative career, were all wasted by this impulsive decision – and yet he knew he could do nothing. A call to the monastery was the only kind of calling which had precedence over the rights of a father. He wrote his son an angry letter, which disowned and clearly shook the young Luther. But his father's anger soon cooled, helped by remembering how the plague had killed two of his other sons, and also by a false report of Luther's own death – compared to that, maybe his becoming a monk was not so bad. In any case, Hans Luder agreed – reluctantly – not to oppose the move.

A year later, Martin took his final vows to become a full Augustinian friar. This, it seemed, was the point of no return. Having indicated his wish to proceed, and the novice master having confirmed that he had satisfactorily completed his novitiate year, the novice allowed the prior to remove his novice's cowl and replace it with the black-and-white habit of the Augustinian order. Placing his hand on an open copy of the order's rule, he then promised obedience to God, to Mary, the mother of Jesus, to the prior, and to a life of poverty and chastity. After more prayers and exhortations, he was ushered to his new seat in the choir, congratulated by his fellow monks, and so began a new life.

The Order of Augustinian Friars

The Order of Augustinian Friars originated in groups of hermits, who lived solitary lives in the mountains and hills of northern Italy in the 13th century. The order was a combination of two monastic traditions. One was the older monastic format of living in monastery buildings. The other was the begging and the theological interests characteristic of the Franciscan and Dominican Friars, who, like the Augustinians, also originated in the 13th century. Augustinian monasteries such as the one in Erfurt combined a strict and ordered lifestyle, with opportunities for intelligent young monks to remain involved in university life. The combination of a serious search for salvation, with the opportunity to continue to study theology in the way with which he had become familiar, made this, out of all the monasteries in Erfurt, exactly what Luther was looking for.

Monastic life

At the time, entry into the monastic life was considered a kind of second baptism. In other words, this was a complete renewal of the Christian life, a new start, and a restoration to an original state of grace, in which purity before God was re-established. This could, of course, be lost through subsequent sin, but it is possible to imagine the elation felt by this new friar as he contemplated a step which seemed to banish his spiritual depression. Despite the lingering sadness of the rupture in the relationship with his father, Luther felt that at last he had found the road to salvation.

Life in the monastery was even more strictly regulated than in the university *bursa* from which he had come. The day was structured around the services held in the monastery chapel, known as the 'canonical hours', in which all 150 Psalms were recited each week. The day began with Matins and Lauds, which entailed being woken in the small hours of the morning. This was followed by the service of Prime at six o'clock in the morning, Terce at nine o'clock, and Sext at noon. After a meal and an hour's rest, the afternoon contained None and Vespers, and Compline rounded off the day after the evening meal. Alongside these, a Mass was said each morning and, at other times, special Masses might be added for a host of different reasons. This meant spending at least six hours a day in church. Apart from this, monks would read (Luther soon started memorizing the Rule of St Augustine), perform various tasks around the monastery, and wander the narrow streets of Erfurt, dressed in the usual black cloak, begging for sustenance. Meals were taken just twice a day, except during Advent and Lent, when once a day sufficed, with dry bread and wine in the evening. At all times, the food was pretty meagre.

Besides the hours in the chapel, a number of other features pervaded the lives of the monks. One was the cold. Only one room of the monastery was heated, and the monks' cells, the chapel and the refectory must have been bitterly cold during the long, icy winters of northern Germany. In winter, the monks were allowed a pair of special slippers, and they could wear animal furs inside their monk's cowl. Yet, in an atmosphere where it was felt that it was especially pleasing to God to endure painful conditions while praying, one can imagine why Luther later recalled how he would often nearly freeze in his cowl during the services. Another factor was the silence, which was imposed for most of the day and night. Meals were held in quiet, apart from the accompaniment of edifying readings from the works of such masters of monastic theology as Bernard of Clairvaux, a 12th-century Cistercian monk, whose writings influenced Luther a great deal in these early years. During these periods of silence, ordinary communications, such as asking for milk or asking the time, had to be done using an agreed sign language.

Neglecting to say the hours (services), or omitting part of the prescribed prayers, was considered a sin by the Augustinian order. So was permitting the eyes to wander during the service, lateness, laughing, grumbling or spilling food. These, however, were considered minor sins. More serious offences were lying, stealing and speaking with a woman. At least once a week, in the daily chapter meeting of the monastery, the monks were encouraged to confess their sins of commission or neglect, and monks could even report on each other's sins. The prior would then impose a suitable punishment, which might often include the saying of further prayers, or recitations of psalms.

Luther took these austerities very seriously. During his first months as a monk, he experienced peace at heart and a sense of at last being pleasing to God. In the monastery library, he held for the first time a full copy of the Bible, which he read eagerly, with fascination and thoroughness. It was not long before he was recognized as a sincere and dedicated monk, if perhaps a little over-scrupulous. He would often fast more than was strictly necessary. Several times he recalled forgetting part of a psalm, or being unsure about whether he had in fact included all the prayers he should, and so he would go back to the chapel to say them all over again, to make sure that he had completed them properly. Confession became an increasingly important part of his life. Monastic spirituality encouraged hunting out the smallest of sins, to ensure that they were fully confessed and that absolution was received. Only thus could the monks be sure they were in a state of grace before God. As one of the more

> 'I almost fasted myself to death, for again and again I went for three days without taking a drop of water or a morsel of food. I was very serious about it.'
>
> **Martin Luther, 'Table Talk', March 1539**

dedicated of the monks, Luther would engage in long bouts of self-examination, once confessing for six hours at a stretch. One of his confessors rebuked him gently for an over-precise nature, suggesting that the sins he kept bringing up were barely sins at all. Luther, however, could not see the point. Were not all sins, small or large, displeasing to God, and potentially fatal to his prospects of salvation?

On his own admission, and from the evidence of his contemporaries, Luther's struggles in the monastery were not the standard temptations. He does not appear to have been abnormally plagued by sexual fantasies, nor was he anxious about money, given his relatively frugal background. Boredom, or *accidie*, was not an especial difficulty, either. Instead, if there was a lingering fear, it was the anxiety over what God really thought of him. We will explore this more in due course.

'I was very pious in the monastery, yet I was sad because I thought God would not be gracious to me. I said Mass and prayed and hardly saw or heard a woman as long as I was in the order.'

Martin Luther, 'Table Talk', spring 1533

Luther's colleagues

Among the 50 or so Augustinian friars in Erfurt, Luther encountered a number of figures who played crucial roles in the drama which would unfold. Johann von Paltz had been Head of Theological Studies in the monastery for the past two decades. Although an argument with colleagues in the order led to his departure soon after Luther's arrival, he was a well-known figure in the theological landscape, and a Professor of Theology in the university. His sermons and theological lectures would urge the right use of the Mass, penance and indulgences (of which more later), through which a true penitence could be achieved with which God would be satisfied. Johann Nathin became Luther's theological tutor after von Paltz left, and even boasted further afield of the new brother's dramatic conversion to the cloister. Johann Lang, who became a close friend and supporter of Luther, and Bartholomäus Arnoldi, who had taught

Luther theology in the university, soon followed him into the monastery as well.

The main influence upon the new young friar was Johann von Staupitz, the Vicar General of the Augustinian Observant Congregation. In this wider role, the Augustinian monastery at Erfurt fell under his jurisdiction, and he was a regular visitor. It was he who, on hearing of Luther's interest in the Bible and his desire to study it, asked for him to be removed from sweeping and cleaning duties, and instead to be set the task of memorizing the whole Bible by heart. This small step accounts for Luther's extraordinary grasp and memory of scripture in the years to come, and had consequences far beyond what Staupitz could ever have imagined.

The priesthood

It was not unusual for a dedicated monk such as Luther to be recommended to prepare for the priesthood. Training consisted primarily in working through the standard late-medieval textbook, the *Sacri Canonis Missae Expositio* (*Exposition of the Sacred Canon of the Mass*) written in 1499 by Gabriel Biel, the famous Tübingen theologian. This was a lengthy and detailed commentary on the liturgy of the Mass, which discussed the key theological questions raised by the different parts of the service. It also advised on the various pastoral problems a priest might encounter arising out of the Mass, such as how to advise people to approach the Mass, or how to cope with feelings of unworthiness.

'The sacrament of the eucharist, as a sacrifice offered to the Most High Father, takes away not only venial but also mortal sin, I do not say only of those who receive it, but, of all those for whom it is offered, so far as concerns guilt and penalty... And therefore this service is offered for the living and the dead.'

Gabriel Biel, *Sacri Canonis Missae Expositio,* **1499**

Here, Luther learned how the Mass did not exactly repeat the sacrifice of Christ fully, but in a lesser way. The priest offered Christ's broken body and blood before God, on behalf of the church, just as Christ had done on Calvary, pleading the merits of his death for their sake. The Mass, wrote Biel, 'kindles love, keeps up the memory of Christ's passion, sustains for the performance of good... cleanses venial sin and sometimes mortal sin... gives the life of grace... fortifies against the falls which are the result of human weakness, and lessens the fire of fleshly lust in the face of the assaults of the devil'. Receiving these benefits, however, depended upon the attitude which a Christian brought to the Mass. To come with only a vague sorrow for sin, or without a sense of love for God in the heart, would lessen the effects of the Mass on the heart. In effect, the Mass was seen as an offering made by the priest to God, to ask for God's help. It was a form of prayer – especially effective prayer at that – which pleased God and merited more of his grace.

Having worked his way through, and taken careful attention of, Biel's work, Luther was finally ordained as a priest in the imposing cathedral in Erfurt on 3 April 1507. The new priest was to celebrate Mass for the first time on 2 May that year. Friends were invited, as was his father, who came with a large retinue from Mansfeld. As the day drew nearer, Luther found himself filled with foreboding at what he was about to do. To handle the very body and blood of Christ, into which the bread and wine was to be transformed, was such a breathtaking thing to do that Luther trembled in his spirit at the prospect.

> 'I was so terrified by the words, "to thee, the eternal, living and true God", that I thought of running away from the altar and said to my prior, "Reverend Father, I'm afraid I must leave the altar." He shouted to me, "Go ahead, faster, faster."'
>
> **Martin Luther, on his first Mass as a priest, 2 May 1507**

During the service, facing the altar in the by now familiar chapel, as he found himself uttering the words, '... we offer unto thee, the living and the true God', Luther suddenly faltered. As he put it later, 'Who am I, that I should lift up my eyes or raise up my hands to the divine Majesty? For I am dust and ashes, and full of sin, and I am speaking to the living, eternal and the true

God!' He whispered his misgivings to the prior of the monastery
who was assisting him, but as these were not unusual emotions
for a new priest, especially one as scrupulous as brother Martin,
the prior advised him to continue nonetheless. These, however,
were not routine utterances of a feigned humility, nor were they
the paranoid fears of a psychologically disturbed neurotic. They
were the natural and inevitable consequence of the medieval
view of the Mass, taken seriously. It may be hard for modern
sensibilities to understand, yet given what Luther and his world
believed about God, the awful judge of humankind, and given
what Biel had taught Luther about the Mass, it
is perhaps not surprising that a thoughtful and
attentive student such as Luther would tremble at
performing such an act.

'I chose 21 saints and
prayed to three every day
when I celebrated Mass...
I prayed especially to the
Blessed Virgin, who with
her womanly heart would
compassionately appease
her Son.'

**Martin Luther, 'Table Talk',
1539**

The day still held one more dramatic
turn. The service over, the new priest and the
congregation retired to a separate room, where
they were to celebrate with wine and rich food.
Perhaps still shaken by his terrifying experience
at the altar, and needing reassurance, he asked
his father whether he was now reconciled to his
son's entry into the monastery and ready to give
his approval. Hans Luder, no longer able to hide
his smouldering resentment, accused Martin in front of the
guests of disobedience to his parents, leaving them to fend for
themselves in their old age. Taken aback, Luther countered
that as God had directly called him out of the thunderclap
at Stotternheim, surely Hans should see this was God's will.
'God grant that it was not an apparition of the devil!' came
the gruff reply.

Fifteen years later, the son admitted that his father's words
'penetrated to the depths of my soul and stayed there'. This God
whom he feared, the God who had apparently called him into
the monastery, the God before whom he had stood trembling at

his first Mass – was he really the good God which Luther longed for him to be, the God of grace and kindness and mercy? Or was he in fact the devil? Was he an angry, remorseless figure, dragging him through doubt, despair and self-torment, before picking up on the slightest excuse to damn him for all eternity? It was a question that demanded a reply.

CHAPTER 2

The Theologian

Martin Luther was now a priest. He began to feel more at ease with the Mass, and found great satisfaction in performing it reverently and well. Aware of his academic background, his superiors in the Augustinian order decided that alongside the canonical hours, and the Masses to be said both in the monastery chapel and in surrounding villages, Luther should continue with his theological studies.

Having gained the status of Master of Arts, Luther was already qualified to lecture on philosophy. Now, more study was needed if he were to qualify to lecture on the Bible. The first step involved studies enabling him to lecture on the *Sentences* of Peter Lombard (c. 1110–60). This central theology textbook of the Middle Ages collected together extracts from scripture and the early church Fathers, arranged under topical headings to facilitate discussion of theological issues. Under the guidance of Johann Nathin, the Augustinian Professor of Theology at the university and a senior member of Luther's order, Luther set to work studying texts such as Gabriel Biel's *Dogmatics*, itself a commentary on Lombard's *Sentences*. He devoured the master's theological ideas, just as he had pored over his commentary on the Mass in preparation for his ordination to the priesthood.

Meanwhile, Johann von Staupitz had been involved with the Elector, Frederick the Wise, in establishing a new university in a small town called Wittenberg, 100 miles north-west of Erfurt. In the winter of 1508–09, he invited Luther to move to teach there. Staupitz was himself Lecturer in Biblical Studies in Wittenberg, so the idea was for Luther to help with the teaching of Aristotle's *Ethics*. At the same time, he would work towards his doctorate, the ultimate qualification to teach theology in the church and university. After just one term, he was recalled to Erfurt for a further two years to fill a gap in the teaching programme, but he eventually returned to Wittenberg in 1512. Brother Luther was placed in charge of the teaching of younger Augustinian friars in the order's house in the town. He received his doctorate on 19 October 1512 and was enrolled as a full teaching member of the university three days later. He was to take over from Staupitz the role of *Lectura in Biblia*, Lecturer in Biblical Studies in the University of Wittenberg, a post in which he remained until he died.

These years also saw the growth of Luther's profile within the Augustinian Order. In 1510, along with a fellow friar, Luther had been sent to Rome to try to sort out a complex internal matter connected with the order. The business trip had been largely unsuccessful, but it did represent Luther's only trip outside Germany in the whole of his life and, despite the fact that he barely mentions it later, an intriguing encounter with the papacy which he was to do so much to undermine.

Luther's theological training

What was Luther taught, and what did he believe? The Middle Ages are sometimes thought of as a period of monolithic certainties, a unified vision of life and society. However, it does not take much delving beneath the surface to realize that this image is far from the truth. Erfurt, like most German universities of the time, was a place of wide theological variety. For several centuries, theology in the universities of Europe had been studied predominantly by what was known as the scholastic method. Scholastic theologians tried to demonstrate that Christian theology made good, rational sense. Scholastics such as Thomas Aquinas (1225–74) were convinced that, while the great truths of Christianity could not always be arrived at by reason, they were nonetheless not fundamentally irrational.

So, in his great work, the *Summa Theologiae*, Aquinas tried not only to show the consistency of Christian doctrine, but also to present it in an orderly and systematic fashion.

A glance at Aquinas's *Summa Theologiae* gives a flavour of the kind of method used. He first states the proposition or question to be debated, for example: 'Was it fitting that Christ be crucified with thieves?' or 'Did Christ set some of the damned free from hell?' He then assembles the evidence against the thesis. Then, with the Latin phrase *sed contra*, he puts the other side of the argument. He finally comes to a conclusion, under the heading *responsio*. Students would be guided through the same method in their university classes, sharpening their skills in debate using this 'dialectical' method of question and answer, submitting propositions to logical analysis. The characteristic product of this process was large tomes of theology, or 'cathedrals of the mind' as they have been called, in which every conceivable question which might be raised concerning the rational coherence of Christianity was addressed, all the way from 'Does God exist?' to 'Could a human miraculously be in several places at the same time?'

By the time Luther came to study, there were three main types of scholastic theology in operation. The first two, following the teaching of Thomas Aquinas and Duns Scotus (c. 1265–1308), were by now collectively known as the *via antiqua*, the 'old way'. Yet alongside this was emerging a new kind of theology, the *via moderna*, the 'modern way'.

Realists and nominalists

The basic distinction between these two *viae* ran along a complex philosophical problem involving the existence of universal concepts. Basically, those in the *via moderna*, known as 'nominalists', did not believe in universal concepts, and those in the *via antiqua* did.

Nominalist thinkers, such as the Englishmen William of Ockham and Robert Holcot, and the Frenchman Pierre d'Ailly, were thought of in more conservative circles as dangerous radical sceptics. They were considered ready to overthrow not only the traditional ideas of universal concepts, but to insist that statements be verified by experience and direct revelation from God in scripture, not just by authority from the past. Here was a whole army of radicals willing to cut down the complex philosophical constructions of high scholasticism, with its abstract ideas of universals and rational logic. 'Ockham's Razor', the idea that the simpler the argument, the better it is, is perhaps the best-known legacy of the movement. Instead of abstract formulations and what seemed to them purely logical games, they preferred simple arguments that could be tested by scientific proof, direct experience and divine revelation.

The problem of 'universals'

Take a collection of different people. You can say that all of them share a particular quality called 'human nature' – which is somehow indefinable, cannot actually be identified in time or space, and yet exists quite apart from the particular people themselves. Such a concept of human nature is called a 'universal', and in the late Middle Ages, people who believed that such universal concepts were real, such as those within both branches of the *via antiqua*, were called 'Realists'. It is possible, however, to deny that such universal concepts exist at all. Some would say that the individual people themselves are all we can be sure of, and the universal concept human nature is irrelevant, unverifiable, unnecessary and non-existent. Such people (and this opinion became more common at the time) were called 'nominalists', believing that such universals existed in name only, not in reality. Human reason was not sufficient to prove or grasp realities beyond what could be seen and touched – these things can be known only if God chooses to reveal them. This was the *via moderna*.

By the time of Luther's arrival at the University of Erfurt, the
Faculty of Theology had become something of a stronghold of the *via moderna*. In a formal disputation of the university in 1497, two professors in the Faculty of Arts who were also to become Luther's main teachers, Jodocus Trutvetter from Eisenach and Bartholomäus Arnoldi from Usingen, had established a coherent programme of teaching, in which nominalist ideas derived from Ockham and Biel were worked through into all areas of the academic curriculum.

There were, however, even more sub-groups within these 'nominalists', which were divided not so much on philosophical lines, but on further theological questions. One central question that medieval theologians often pondered concerned the parts played by God and humans in salvation, the question of how we can come into a right relationship with God or, as the theologians called it, the doctrine of justification. Contrary to what we might think, no one in late-medieval theological circles believed that a person could earn salvation purely by their own efforts. All agreed that God's grace was necessary if salvation was to be won. The point at issue was how much and what kind of help was needed, and what part, if any, men and women must play in the process. The church's official teaching on this vital question was far from clear, and a number of different positions were held, not least among the nominalist faction of late-medieval theology.

> 'Thus God has established the rule (covenant) that whoever turns to him and does what he can will receive forgiveness of sins from God. God infuses grace into such a man, who is thus taken back into friendship.'
>
> **Gabriel Biel, *The Circumcision of the Lord*, c. 1460**

One group of nominalists included figures such as Gregory of Rimini and Hugolino of Orvieto, who took their cue from the great fifth-century Bishop of Hippo in North Africa, St Augustine. They were 'nominalist' on the question of universal concepts, but when it came to the Christian doctrine of justification, they held that humankind was basically helpless. Only God himself, by his sovereign mercy, could intervene and save people. Another group of nominalists, however (and here we come to those who more directly influenced Luther, such as William of Ockham and Gabriel Biel), thought that there was something which could be done to initiate the process of salvation.

When Luther read Biel's textbook of dogmatic theology, he came across and was persuaded by the idea that God has entered into a covenant, or pact, with humanity. Essentially, if the sinner did what lay within him (the Latin phrase was *quod in se est*), then God would not deny him his grace. Within the framework of this agreement or covenant, sinners were capable of making a small moral effort on their own, without the help of God's grace. This initial effort was required before God would respond. This might involve feeling a genuine sorrow for sin, or generating a sense of love for God. In response to this, God would give a supply ('infusion' was the technical term) of his grace to help fan this spark into a flame. This initial gift of grace was not enough to merit salvation on its own, however. The Christian then had to cooperate with God's grace and, by the exercise of good works done with God's help, perfect this contrition for sin and love for God, so that salvation could truly be merited.

This exploration into some of the complicated paths of late-medieval theology may seem unnecessary, but it helps us to grasp the nature of Luther's early theological training. These were the ideas he encountered in the Erfurt lectures of Trutvetter and Arnoldi, and was reading in the works of Ockham and Biel. Their effect was to reinforce the sense that to be saved meant achieving a true sorrow for his many sins, and a love for God, not for selfish reasons, but for God's own sake. It encouraged self-examination, peering into his own motivations and actions to discover whether he really was contrite, whether he really did love God, and whether he was active enough in good works which would gradually purge the soul, ready for heaven. The monk who agonized over his fitness to perform the Mass found in this theology a confirmation of such uncertainty.

Back to the future

At the same time as all this, another movement with its origins in the 15th century cast scorn on all these varieties of scholastic thought. By the time Luther was studying theology, the Renaissance, which had begun in northern Italy, had spread northwards. As it extended into Germany, the Netherlands and England, it captured the allegiance of many younger scholars, with its exhilarating programme of returning to the sources of ancient classical Greece and Rome as a model for literature, art, architecture, law and rhetoric.

'Humanism', as this educational and cultural programme became known, is not to be confused with modern humanism, which is normally atheistic. While it did have a high view of human dignity, the 16th-century version was mostly religious in character. It was not so much a set of ideas or philosophical opinions, but rather a trend or a taste for all things classical. The great motivating desire was to acquire eloquence and skill with words and language. So, everything was devoted towards a new kind of education, which involved making the study of classical texts possible – as these were thought the best models of eloquence available. These texts could be Greek literature, Roman law, classical poetry or early Christian theology. Thus, the humanists promoted vigorously the study of Greek and Hebrew, alongside Latin, which was, of course, the language of all scholarly work in the Middle Ages, so that these texts could be read in the original, avoiding what they felt was the misleading filter of medieval translations.

The humanist ideal

Humanists valued education, and especially ancient languages, very highly, as shown in this excerpt from François Rabelais's *On Education* (c. 1532):

It is my earnest desire that you shall become a perfect master of languages. First of Greek, as Quintilian advises, secondly of Latin; and then of Hebrew, on account of the holy scriptures; also of Chaldean and Arabic, for the same reason; and I would have you model your Greek style on Plato's and your Latin on that of Cicero. Keep your memory well stocked with every tale from history... Of the liberal arts, geometry, arithmetic, and music, I gave you some when you were still small, at the age of five or six. Go on and learn the rest, also the rules of astronomy.

Humanists took particular exception to the methods and products of scholastic theology, of whatever kind. They felt that the scholastic method encouraged the asking and answering of a whole series of irrelevant questions. After all, did it really matter whether a body could in theory be in several places at once? Or whether the Son of God could have become incarnate as an animal? They also objected strongly to the method of using medieval commentaries or selections, rather than the original ancient texts themselves. For a humanist, these lengthy, turgid medieval interpretations simply got in the way of the brilliance of the original authors, like a tangled swathe of brambles covering up a field, which needed clearing away. Humanists wanted a direct encounter with the original text of classical authors, the Bible and the Fathers, rather than have this muddied by an extra layer of explanations made by lesser, more recent men, writing in crude and verbose medieval Latin.

> You'd extricate yourself faster from a labyrinth than from the tortuous obscurities of realists, nominalists, Thomists, Albertists, Ockhamists and Scotists.'
>
> **Desiderius Erasmus, *In Praise of Folly*, 1509**

So, using the recent invention of mass-type printing,

humanists were responsible for the republication of a whole series of ancient Christian texts, which made a new kind of scholarship possible. Three works in particular were important for our story.

In 1503, Desiderius Erasmus, soon to become the most famous humanist of them all, published the first edition of his *Enchiridion Militis Christiani* (*Handbook of the Christian Soldier*). Although Erasmus's *Enchiridion* did not really become widely known until after its third print-run in 1515, it laid out a very important programme of reform in the church. Erasmus, like many humanists, was impatient – not only with the theology of the medieval schools, but also with the general state of the church, and the clergy in particular. The clergy, he wrote, were 'so universally loathed that even a chance meeting is said to be ill-omened… they believe it's the highest form of piety to be so uneducated that they can't even read.' The *Enchiridion* put forward two significant suggestions for the reform of the church. The first was a collective return to the scriptures and the writings of the early Fathers. Erasmus's proposal was to abandon the infested waters of medieval theology in favour of the fresh springs of scriptural and early church theology. The second was that hope for the future lay more with the laity than the clergy. The key was the renewal and education of a whole generation of laypeople, who would bring about a revitalization of the whole church.

Desiderius Erasmus

Desiderius Erasmus was born in Rotterdam in about 1467, the illegitimate child of a priest. He joined a monastery, but left, with permission, for Paris in 1495. Throughout his life he travelled widely, becoming a professor in Cambridge from 1509 to 1516, eventually settling in Basel in 1521. Later, in 1529, he moved to Catholic Freiburg when Basel become too Reformed for his liking. Returning to Basel later, he died in 1536. Erasmus was a key figure in the Renaissance in Northern Europe and the best-known humanist scholar of his day. His chief desire was to see the Christian faith renewed through good education and scholarship, rejecting the obscurantist methods of scholasticism. Among his most famous works were *In Praise of Folly* (1509), a satire upon the failings of the medieval church, the *Enchiridion* (1503) and his edition of the Greek New Testament (1516).

In 1506, three years after the publication of the *Enchiridion*, the 11-volume *Amerbach Edition* of the works of Augustine finally appeared. For the first time for centuries, it was possible to read the greatest authority in Western theology in full, in context, and without the help of medieval commentators, whose 'glosses' in the standard selections on offer made sure that any inquisitive reader would interpret the master in the 'correct' way. This again began to have a revolutionary effect, as scholars began to realize that the way in which Augustine had been interpreted by the scholastics was not as accurate as it had seemed.

Most significant, however, was Erasmus's greatest achievement, his *Novum Instrumentum*, an edition of the Greek New Testament published in 1516. Although this edition was not as reliable as it might have been – Erasmus only had a limited number of Greek texts to work from – it became the first-ever printed edition of the Greek text, so that, for the first time, theologians all over Europe had the chance to compare the standard Latin Bible text, the *Vulgate*, or 'common text' of St Jerome, dating back to the fourth century, with the original. A number of disturbing things emerged. For example, medieval theologians were unanimous in seeing marriage as a full sacrament of the church, alongside holy communion, baptism and four others, on the basis of Jerome's translation of Ephesians 5:32, which referred to it as a *sacramentum*. When Erasmus's edition appeared, it became clear that the original Greek word really meant 'mystery'. The scriptural basis for regarding marriage as equal in value to baptism and the eucharist was profoundly shaken. Hence, the work of Erasmus and the other humanists played a large part in loosening the hold of the

church's traditional authority in the minds of many educated
and literate laypeople. When this edition came out, Luther
lapped it up greedily, quoting from it in his commentaries from
1516 onwards.

While not engaged in open warfare, scholasticism and
humanism jostled uncomfortably in the lecture halls and
curricula of universities across Germany in the early years of
the 16th century. And Erfurt was no exception. The two schools
of thought were both present in the university, although
relationships between them were, on the whole, fairly good.
Johann Jäger, one of Luther's friends in the *bursa* where
he lodged as a student, was later to be a significant figure in
Erfurt humanism. As was the fashion among humanists, he
took a Latinized name, Crotus Rubianus, and later commented
admiringly on Luther as a fine example of a young humanist
scholar. Luther was known for his knowledge of classical writers.
He probably attended lecture courses by humanist teachers,
and knew many students attracted to humanism. Luther gained
from them a knowledge of classical authors, which he would
quote throughout his life – even when he entered the monastery
he made sure he took with him a copy of Virgil's poetry.

Yet when it came to theology, Luther's mind was decisively
shaped by his nominalist teachers. After his entry into the
monastery, tensions between humanists and scholastics
grew, after an attack in 1506 on the teaching methods of the
university by the combative humanists Nicholas Marschalk
(who, like Luther, later moved to Wittenberg) and Mutian
Rufus, who became a big player in the Erfurt academic scene
from 1511. By the time humanism became a significant rival
to scholasticism in Erfurt, however, Luther's interests lay
elsewhere, in the salvation of his soul within the walls of the
Augustinian monastery, and subsequently in the new University
of Wittenberg. During the time of Luther's studies in Erfurt, the
kind of humanism on offer there was of a gentler, less abrasive

kind. While Luther must have known about it and spoken its language to an extent, it seems to have left little mark on the theology of the young scholar – apart, of course, from the precious gifts of the original text of the Bible and Augustine, the key tools with which he would later attack the papacy.

Growing doubts

These were the contours of the theological landscape at the time that Luther's mind was being formed. Taught theology by nominalists, Luther, too, believed that as long as he did his best, God would give him grace to help him to become better. Humanist texts were allowing him to study the great authorities of the Bible and the Fathers with fresh eyes. From 1509–10, he studied Augustine's works and Lombard's *Sentences*, and some of the notes he made in the margins of these works have survived to this day. They show him to be a not particularly original adherent of the theology of the *via moderna*. He had followed his teachers well, and there was little sign at this stage of any distinctive departure from them.

> 'When I was busy with public lecturing and writing I often accumulated my appointed prayers for a whole week, or even two or three weeks. Then I would take a Saturday off, or shut myself in for as long as three days without food or drink, until I had said the prescribed prayers.'
>
> **Martin Luther, 'Table Talk', 1533**

Luther's own timetable, however, was becoming almost unworkable. Besides the canonical hours, he now had to say Mass in the friary chapel and in the surrounding villages when required, and to pursue a punishing programme of theological study. He would often have to skip saying the hours to attend lectures, resolving to make them up in his own time. The backlog became more and more onerous until, at one stage, he was many weeks behind in his devotions.

As we have seen, even from before his time in the monastery, Luther had been plagued by periods of depression or despair. At these times, he wondered whether God really did hold good intentions towards him or not, sensing particularly keenly the

stare of Christ the judge, standing over him, demanding an impossible level of inner purity. He wondered whether these feelings were evidence that he was not one of the chosen at all, but that he was, in fact, among those destined to be damned to eternal suffering. These experiences, by no means unusual, although felt more intensely by Luther than most, were known as *Anfechtungen*, a German word which is difficult to translate, but which means something stronger than temptation or trial, nearer to 'assault' or 'attack'. It seemed that in these experiences, for some reason which he was only later to identify, God himself was assaulting Luther, subjecting him to the most terrifying ordeal.

There was, of course, a whole science of late-medieval pastoral practice which was meant to deal with precisely this kind of thing. In particular, there was the sacrament of penance. The penitential system was a cyclical process whereby Christians who fell into sin could be restored to a state of grace. When a medieval Christian sinned, he or she would go to a priest to confess that sin. On the condition that the sinner was truly contrite, and was seeking God's help out of love for God, the priest would pronounce forgiveness, or absolution, on the further condition that certain acts of 'satisfaction', which were meant to prove the authenticity of the sinner's repentance, were fulfilled. These acts could be saying a set number of prayers, going on a short pilgrimage, or other acts of contrition. When these acts were performed, then the sinner was restored to a state of grace, which would be maintained until he or she sinned once more, when the cycle would start all over again. This process was intended to offer psychological and spiritual consolation to precisely the kind of sinner Luther was, burdened by a sense of doubt or despair over their unworthiness to come before God.

In a way, this was the popular manifestation of Biel's theology of justification or, more correctly, Biel's theology was designed to provide a theological basis for this pastoral practice. Luther's growing problem, however, was with the conditions. Was he really contrite about his sins? Or, hidden away in the dark recesses of his heart, did he secretly enjoy his sins so much that he continued to commit them again and again? Did he really have a pure love for God, or was his love for God selfish, just for what he could get out of it? For sin to be forgiven, it needed to be confessed, but could he actually remember all his most minute sins? Might he have forgotten some sins, which would, of course, then remain unconfessed and unforgiven, leaving him under God's severe wrath? More painfully still, how could he *love* this God who seemed an inscrutable judge, demanding from him what he could not provide?

The manuals of pastoral counselling of the time advised priests to comfort anxious penitents such as Luther with the news that an exact following of the rules was not necessary for those of tender conscience. However, this did not really help. The rules might be relaxed, but what about the heart? Even if he had kept the rules, if he still failed to produce a pure love for God, then he would still have satisfied neither God nor himself. So, the sacrament of penance, although intended to offer help, in fact made things worse. It promised relief if only certain conditions were met, but the young friar was increasingly doubtful of whether he could meet those conditions at all.

The monastic atmosphere

On the shelves of the library of the Augustinian friary in Erfurt lay copies of several works by Bernard of Clairvaux. Bernard was something of a hero to monks such as Luther and his colleagues in Erfurt, having developed a rich spiritual theology in the 12th century, and offering a wide range of advice on the spiritual life. Luther took these books down and read them, and he would have heard them recited out loud over meals in the refectory, too. As his fellow monks read out these long Latin sermons, Luther noticed Bernard's close attention to scripture, and a piety

which returned again and again to the sufferings and humility
of Jesus. Bernard advised his hearers to meditate regularly
and often on the cross of Christ, especially when perplexed or
anxious, and one of the chief prizes to be gained from this was
the virtue of humility. Humility was the virtue which God valued
most. Bernard explained how its abiding image was found in
the crucified Jesus, and how God regularly seemed to use the
experience of suffering and doubt to bring about humility in the
human soul. The Christian was, therefore, to become like the
crucified Christ: humble, passive and surrendered to God.

These themes made a deep impression on the young
brother Martin. Bernard was not the only one to turn his
thoughts increasingly to the crucified Jesus. Both
Johann von Paltz, the Professor of Theology in
the University of Erfurt, and Johann von Staupitz,
Luther's superior in the order, had in different
ways urged meditation on the cross as the answer
to religious scruples, doubts and anxieties. During
their long conversations over Luther's spiritual
struggles, Staupitz had also advised the young
monk to look to the crucified Christ for consolation
in his temptations. Luther began to find some
comfort in thinking about the sufferings of Christ

'It is the greatest
foolishness to think sins
may be greater than
God's mercy.'

**Johann von Staupitz, Luther's
superior in the Augustinian
order, from a sermon, 1516**

on the cross. It led him to take his attention off his own sins or
virtues, and to look instead to the sufferings of Christ as the key
to his salvation.

'At war within myself'

Luther is usually thought to have completely rejected medieval
Catholic Christianity, replacing it with an entirely new brand.
This is only half true. He clearly rejected some aspects of
medieval scholastic thought, but his theology is a strong
reaffirmation of vital elements of late-medieval *spirituality*. He
could not have crafted the theology he did without the help of

Bernard of Clairvaux, Johann Tauler, Johann von Staupitz and other key figures in the medieval theological landscape. Luther was more of a Catholic than he is often given credit for.

Some remarks Luther made when looking back on his struggles give us a window into his heart at this point in his life. He wrote about how he felt 'at war within himself'. In the monastery, the young Luther breathed a spirituality which made him constantly examine himself, remember his sins and unworthiness, and despair of his own abilities to be good enough for God. On the other hand, in his theological studies, he was being advised to 'do what lay within him', to make a good confession, to try to be contrite for his sins, to hope that his own effort at loving God would be sincere enough to merit the gift of God's grace, which would help him become what God demanded he should become. The spiritual atmosphere of the monastery seemed to be at odds with the advice of the theologians. A spirituality of self-accusation lived uncomfortably alongside a theology of self-justification. One of them had to give way. In the end, it was the theology Luther had learnt from his masters at Erfurt which was found to be wanting. Luther took up many of the themes he had encountered in Bernard of Clairvaux's writings, in the long conversations in Staupitz's study, in the popular sermons which invited congregations to meditate on the sufferings of Jesus on the cross. Armed with all of these, and shaped by his close reading of the Bible and the works of Augustine, Luther slowly developed a theology which was to shake the medieval church to its foundations in the years ahead.

CHAPTER 3

The Discovery

After Erfurt, Wittenberg must have seemed the back of beyond. It had nothing remotely to compare with the grandeur of the cathedral in which Luther had been ordained, or the antiquity of the university he had left behind. Compared to Erfurt's 36 churches, Wittenberg had just two, and a few small chapels. When Luther arrived there, leaving behind the gentle rolling hills of Thuringia for the bleak flatlands of Saxony, he found a city occupying a small triangular rise beside the River Elbe, about a mile long and half a mile across at its widest point. Scattered within the city walls rose about 400 houses, with at the most 3,000 inhabitants, compared with Erfurt's 20,000. The streets were dirty, the houses mud-built, with roofs of hay and straw, and the Augustinian monastery which was to be his home, just inside the walls at the eastern edge of the city, was still only partially built.

However, Wittenberg had two significant advantages. First, it was the capital of Electoral Saxony, which was one of the most powerful of the territorial German states. The key figure in the area was the shy but steady Elector of the region, Frederick the Wise (1463–1525). A pious and educated man, he was an avid collector of relics of the saints. In 1490 Frederick had begun to develop the town. Beginning with the restoration of the castle at the western end of the city, he built a church attached to it. By the time of Luther's arrival, 64 priests used to say the daily Requiem Masses there. After 1503, it functioned as the university church. This church held Frederick's large collection of relics, including a thorn from Christ's 'crown' and a thumb of St Anne, the mother of the

Virgin Mary, purchased by Frederick on a recent pilgrimage to Palestine. By 1520, the collection held around 19,000 items, and had for some while been a popular destination for those wishing to gain indulgences, or relaxation of punishments to be endured in purgatory, the place where the dead were said to be purged of their remaining sins. These indulgences were available to visitors who had seen or touched them.

Second, it had a university. Until recently, Electoral Saxony did not have its own university to compare with those in other states. So, in 1502, Frederick had sought and received permission from the emperor (papal recognition followed five years later) to found a new university in the town. The new University of Wittenberg was thus his pride and joy, and he would defend its members to the hilt. Despite never fully adopting Luther's ideas, the patronage and backing of this key political figure became vital for Luther throughout the coming stormy years.

So, despite its scruffy appearance and size, Wittenberg was a strategic place. The university had brought status and prosperity to the city, and so Luther's final move there in 1512, while on one level an academic step downwards from the grandeur of Erfurt, on another level was a move to the political centre of his world.

By 1512 about 200 students matriculated each year. Here, too, Luther found humanists and scholastics on the teaching staff of the university. Luther's main colleagues in the theology faculty were Petrus Lupinus, a scholastic follower of the 13th-century theologian Duns Scotus, Nicholas von Amsdorf, who was Staupitz's nephew and in time became a close friend and supporter of Luther, and Andreas Bodenstein von Karlstadt, who was a follower of Thomas Aquinas and a passionate figure who came to play a significant part in the drama soon to unfold.

'Five particles of the milk of the Virgin Mary... Four pieces of the hair of Mary... 13 pieces of the manger of Jesus... Two pieces of the hay... One piece of the burning bush which Moses saw.'

Official catalogue of relics in Wittenberg's Castle Church

Luther moved into the Augustinian monastery in Wittenberg, which had been founded only recently in 1502. It was a large building where at any one time about 50 brothers would stay, some combining monastic life with their studies within the university, just as Luther had done at Erfurt. Luther initially occupied a small cell on the ground floor, and each day would move between the basement, where the refectory served meals for the brothers, and the middle floor, where he would lecture in halls used by the university.

The empire

As the Roman empire disintegrated under waves of attacks by various barbarian tribes in the fifth and sixth centuries AD, Europe descended into a period of political and civil instability. However, dreams of empire still survived. In AD 800, Pope Leo III crowned Charlemagne, the Frankish king, as 'Emperor of the Romans' – this was the beginning of the *Holy* Roman Empire. Centuries of dispute followed between popes and emperors as to which held true power in Europe. By the 15th century, the empire had changed hands and was now more focused in northern Europe, with a few territories in northern Italy. Thus, it was increasingly referred to as the 'Holy Roman Empire of the German Nation'. By the 16th century, the empire was in the hands of the Habsburg family, who now ruled a patchwork of states and 'free imperial cities' over a wide area of central Europe, and was one of the larger powers in the late Middle Ages, alongside the kings of France, England, Spain and, of course, the pope. The imperial estates, (local rulers who owed allegiance to the emperor) and Electors (seven regional princes who chose new emperors) met together at 'Diets', which conducted the business and decided the policy of the empire. The emperor sat as the arbitrator and representative of the whole empire above the individual estates.

During these early years after his return to Wittenberg in 1512, Luther set to lecturing on the book of the Bible he knew best from long hours of recitation in the monastery: the book of Psalms. From 1513–15, for two hours each week, starting at six o'clock in the morning, he worked his way through each of the 150 psalms. He ensured that his students had printed copies of the text, with generous spaces in the margins, and spaces between the lines, for copying notes. He would begin by explaining the meaning of contested words, so students could insert their meanings as 'glosses' between or beside the lines, and then he would proceed with a full exposition of the psalm in question. The notes from these lectures, only comparatively recently discovered, give us an insight into Luther's own thinking at this time. Here, we see him reflecting the characteristic themes of the *via moderna*. Here are the familiar notes he had learnt from Gabriel Biel – 'doing what is within him', the 'covenant' God has established, which guarantees the gift of grace, provided men and women fulfil certain conditions.

> 'Hence the teachers correctly say that to a man who does what is within him God gives grace without fail... because of this promise of God and the covenant of his mercy.'
>
> **Martin Luther, First Psalms Commentary, 1513–15**

However, although the familiar notes of the old theology are still audible, as we follow these lectures through carefully, it is possible to hear the first strains of a new kind of music, sounding for the first time in Luther's mind. As he read the psalmists' prayers of despair and anxious cries to God for mercy, he saw in them an echo of what was happening in his own soul, and began to find in them an answer to his own restless striving. Luther saw in these cries for help the work of God, humbling these sinners, bringing them to the point where they know they have nothing left to offer. In a secret, hidden and surprising way, God is working through the experience of anguish to bring about the salvation of these people. They seem to be in the pits of despair, desperately crying out to God for mercy, despised

by their friends and enemies – yet in all this God is working to
bring about the state of mind needed to receive his gifts. God
achieves his purposes through suffering, pain and anxiety. Yet,
of course, these are not the things in which you expect to find
God. As a result, most people do not recognize this as God's
work, because they expect God only to be revealed in glory and
splendour. The way God works confounds human expectations,
and so faith is needed to see past the appearance of things to
their true reality.

Already we can hear some themes which sound different
from the theology Luther had learned. Humility, for example –
a central theme in these lectures, and a commonly prized asset
for a monk – was normally thought of as a virtue, a positive and
admirable quality to be possessed, which God would reward with
grace. Yet Luther begins to see it differently. For him, humility
is not so much a positive virtue to be acquired, as the sheer
absence of pride and self-confidence. He associates it with
words such as 'emptiness', 'nothingness' and 'self-accusation'.
It is not so much the presence of something as the absence of
something – it is the despair of yourself which arises when you
come to the end of your own resources, and realize you have
nothing left to give. It is not the person who seems to possess
the virtue of humility who will be justified, but the person who
despairs of his own virtue altogether.

As he worked his way through the Psalms, it also seems
that Luther arrived at a new understanding of the significance
of the death of Christ. Late-medieval theology and piety was
saturated with images of the cross. It was normal to understand
the cross as the means by which God chose to save the world
– Christ died to satisfy the justice of God, which demanded a
price be paid as a result of human sin, as the great St Anselm
had taught. It could also be seen as an example to be imitated
– sinners are to imitate Christ's suffering and humility. Or it
could be represented as a spur to devotion – by contemplating
Jesus on the cross, you were made to feel an intense sympathy

for him, a deep sorrow for the sins which put him there, and resolve to try not to commit them again.

Luther, however, goes beyond all this. For him, the cross of Christ reveals God's characteristic way of working in the world. God condemns before he saves. If God is to be able to save him, he must be brought to a sense of his own powerlessness before his creator. He can only come with empty hands. God reveals this pattern in the cross, where Christ, too, is made helpless, before he is raised from death. On the cross, Christ seems to be suffering defeat, yet to the eye of faith, God is working out the salvation of the world. God does a 'strange or alien work' (subjecting the Christian to doubt, despair and suffering) in order to achieve his true purpose, his 'proper work', that of justifying the sinner. What seems to be valuable – namely, human religious activity, wisdom or philosophy – is, in fact, worthless. And what seems detestable and negligible – the experience of suffering, temptation, awareness of sin and failure – is, in fact, God's precious work to humble and then save the sinner. This was Luther's emerging 'theology of the cross'.

> 'He went before you, carrying his cross, and on the cross he died for you, so that you too should carry your cross, and long for a death on the cross. For if you share his death, you will also share his life'
>
> **Thomas à Kempis,** *The Imitation of Christ,* c. 1430

This new understanding of the cross seems to have begun to help to resolve Luther's spiritual struggles. All the contrition, self-accusation and awareness of sin, which late-medieval spirituality evoked in a monk such as Luther, originally seemed to him a barrier to his acceptance by God. If he had nothing he could offer to God, how could it help him to be told that if he only did what lay within him, then God would give him his grace? What if he did not do it? What if he did not love God for God's own sake, or hate his sins? What if he secretly hated this God who demanded so much? This new understanding of the cross as the revelation of God's way with sinners taught him a new meaning to his experience of despair about himself. Far from a disqualification from grace, it became in fact the only qualification for it. As

Luther later put it, 'God only saves sinners, only teaches the stupid, only enriches the poor, only raises the dead.' Therefore, to be saved one must become sinful, foolish, poor and helpless – exactly what his spirituality had led Luther to acknowledge himself to be.

Growing responsibility

In addition to lecturing, Luther was soon promoted from the position of sub-prior of the Wittenberg monastery to District Vicar, with oversight of 11 different Augustinian monasteries, including his old monastic home at Erfurt. His duties included visiting them regularly, stepping in when there was any trouble to resolve, even extending to oversight of budgetary matters, such as how much a monastery spent on wine, bread, meat and beer on special occasions, such as saints' days. Several times a week, Luther would make his way out of the monastery along the main street towards the *Stadtkirche*, the city church which stood on the highest point of the city and served as the main parish church for the inhabitants. He soon became not just a regular, but also the most popular, preacher there. Some theologians seem very different in the pulpit than in the lecture hall; Luther was much the same in both. These early sermons sound the same chords as his lectures on the Psalms – the themes of the cross and of 'humility, in which a man recognizes his own nothingness and leaves all good to God, not daring to claim anything for himself'.

This period in Wittenberg, from 1512 to 1518, was the most vital and creative of Luther's life. Over this time, as he lectured day in and day out to his students in Wittenberg, he gradually developed a new type of theology, which slowly but surely moved away from the theology of his teachers. After finishing his marathon lecture series on the Psalms, Luther took on St Paul's letter to the Romans. Every Monday and Friday morning between spring 1515 and autumn 1516, he walked into the lecture hall, armed with his copy of the text, printed out, as the Psalms had been, with lots of space for 'glosses' to be dictated to his hearers. After that, he turned to the book of Hebrews and then Paul's letter to the Galatians. By the end of this period, Luther had quite clearly broken with some of the main ideas of the *via moderna* in which he had been trained. By now, he was feeling confident that the way pointed out by Gabriel Biel and his teachers at Erfurt was nothing but a blind alley. Yet this was no erudite academic theological shift. It was a profoundly personal discovery.

Making a break

'But they who deem themselves just and wise and think they are somebody are most violently hostile to this alien work, which is the cross of Christ and our Adam... So they do not come to God's proper work, which is justification or the resurrection of Christ.'

Martin Luther, in a sermon on St Thomas's Day, 1516

Much later, in 1545, when Luther was writing a preface to the first complete edition of his Latin works, he reflected back on this period, and the crucial developments it held.

The 'Autobiographical Fragment' refers to an experience which has sometimes been called Luther's 'Reformation breakthrough' or 'tower experience', due to another occasion on which Luther mentioned that he made his vital theological discovery in a heated room in the tower of the Augustinian monastery in Wittenberg. Scholars of Luther have argued for centuries about when this breakthrough took place, and there is no sign that any clear consensus has been reached. The slight majority think that at some point about 1514 and 1515, while living in the monastery at Wittenberg, and pursuing his daily round of lecturing, praying, preaching, letter writing and studying, Luther took a vital step forward when he discovered a new meaning to the term 'righteousness of God'.

Biel and all the theologians Luther had studied before had led him to believe that the 'righteousness of God' (*iustitia dei*) meant something like God's 'justice'. In other words, it

referred to the awesome and uncompromising justice of God, which demanded perfection and could only spell bad news for sinners, who, in God's court of law, deserved only punishment. This is why Luther says he 'hated' the phrase, feeling a slump of despondency whenever he read it. Yet as he pored over these words from St Paul, it began to dawn on him that they could be read in another way altogether. Rather than indicating God's justice by which sinners were pronounced guilty, God's 'righteousness' was a gift he gave to sinners, which meant they instantly possessed the righteousness God required. In Latin, the word *iustitia* can mean both 'righteousness' and 'justification'. So when Luther writes of how 'the merciful God justifies us by faith', he means that God makes us righteous. His righteousness is not the standard by which we are judged guilty, but instead is something given to us as a gift. Rather than demanding that we produce what is required, he gives what is required as a completely free gift. Of course, if it is a gift, it cannot be earned; it can only be gratefully received. And the means by which it is received is faith.

The crucial notion of faith is often misunderstood. Sometimes faith is thought of as a positive quality, something difficult to achieve, a bit like a kind of psychic power, which some people have and some do not. Nothing could be further from Luther's understanding of what faith is. For him, faith is defined by its object. Faith on its own can do nothing. In fact, it might be better to translate the Latin word *fides* with the English word 'trust'; it means trusting that when God declares in the gospel that he justifies the ungodly, not the godly (Romans 5:8), then that is precisely what he does. Faith is simply 'taking God at his word', refusing to try to impress God by religious or humanitarian acts but, instead, taking it as read that God loves, forgives and welcomes those who know that they do not deserve it, purely because God says so.

Luther's 'Autobiographical Fragment' (1545)

*I had conceived a burning desire to understand what Paul meant in
his Letter to the Romans, but thus far there had stood in my way, not
'coldness of the blood', but that one phrase which is in chapter one:
'The righteousness of God is revealed in it.' I hated that phrase, 'the
righteousness of God...' I did not love, no, rather I hated this righteous God
who punishes sinners. In silence, if I did not blaspheme, then certainly I
grumbled vehemently and got angry at God...*

*I meditated night and day on those words until at last, by the mercy
of God, I paid attention to their context: 'The righteousness of God is
revealed in it, as it is written: "The just person lives by faith."' I began to
understand that in this verse the righteousness of God is that by which the
righteous man lives by the gift of God, in other words by faith; and that
this sentence, 'the righteousness of God is revealed', refers to a passive
righteousness, i.e. that by which the merciful God justifies us by faith, as
it is written: 'The righteous person lives by faith.' This immediately made
me feel as if I had been born again and entered through open gates into
paradise itself.*

For Luther, there are two ways to try to establish a relationship
with God. One is by what he calls 'works'. In this way, we bring
before God all the things that should make him pleased with
us – our prayers, humility, sorrow for sin, religious attendance,
acts of generosity and so on. And on the basis of these we hope
that God will look with favour on us and help us to be better.
This way, according to Luther, is doomed to failure. He had
tried it for many years and, tragically, it was the way he felt
had been recommended by almost all the popular forms of
piety and theology in the church of his day. All the language of
'doing what lay within you', having a 'good intention', however
qualified by the theologians, was none other than trying to be
justified, made righteous by works. Not only was it doomed to

failure, it was also a recipe for anxiety and frenetic activity. You could never know if you had done enough, whether your love for God was pure enough, or your hatred for sin sincere enough. As a result, the Christian life was destined either to be an exercise in delusion, smugly assuming that your own efforts were good enough to impress God, or frustration, never knowing whether you had done enough to merit God's grace.

The second way, however, was a relationship based on faith or, better still, trust. Its basis was not human effort, but God's declaration of love, forgiveness and favour, which God gave in sending Christ into the world. Christians are simply to trust that God overlooks their sins, that they are loved, forgiven and welcomed, despite those very sins. Most late-medieval understandings of justification saw it as a kind of process, whereby people gradually became more righteous and less sinful. As they cooperate with God's grace working in them, the sinful part gets smaller and the righteous part becomes larger, until one day, usually after many years in purgatory, the place of 'purging', sin is removed altogether. Only then, so it was thought, would they be fully justified and free to enter God's presence. Luther proposed a strikingly different understanding of justification. Instead of being 'partly sinful and partly righteous', Christians are, according to Luther, 'at the same time righteous and sinful'. In themselves, they remain sinners, with all kinds of mixed motives, wrong desires and selfish acts. Yet, by virtue of the righteousness of Christ, given and received by faith, they are seen by God now as they one day will be: pure, righteous and forgiven.

> 'Luther's conflicts... reached their crisis in the question: "How can this God be just?"'
>
> **Bernhard Lohse,** *Martin Luther's Theology*, **1999**

This 'faith', however, is not a facile, easy thing. Luther acknowledged a natural human inclination to want to impress God, others and ourselves with our goodness. To have this declared as worthless, to have every achievement and honour cast from our hands is a devastating thing yet, until this happens, we do not tend to learn faith. If we come with hands full of our own goodness, we cannot have the empty hands necessary to receive the gift of Christ's righteousness. For Luther, God does not want our goodness – he simply wants our trust. Here, his earlier thoughts about humility and about how God uses suffering to bring us to an awareness of our bankruptcy before him, merged with this new understanding of faith.

In the 'Autobiographical Fragment', even at the distance of some 30 years after the event, Luther still remembers the exuberant sense of relief and joy he felt on making this discovery. No longer did he have to be anxious, wondering if he was sincere enough in his love for God. The God who had been a tyrant, a demanding, condemning God, was suddenly transformed for Luther into a good, generous, big-hearted God, whom he could genuinely love, rather than secretly hate. He had found a good and gracious God.

As Luther saw it, such faith could not help but lead on to a transformed life. As he put it to his students while lecturing on the book of Romans, 'We are not made righteous by doing righteous works; but rather we do righteous works by being made righteous.' Luther's experience told him that the emotional and physical energy put into religious activity, such as the saying of the hours in the monastery, the intensity of detailed confession and the hours of fasting in Lent, tended to leave precious little time or energy for genuine works of kindness or love to one's neighbour. Freed from the intensity of these demands, he now felt that he and all those who grasped this new understanding of 'justification by grace through faith', would be more, not less, inclined to be good neighbours, citizens and Christians. Moreover, these 'works' would now be genuinely pleasing to God, as they were not performed out of

> 'Faith is a living, bold trust in God's grace, so certain of God's favour that it would risk death a thousand times trusting in it. Such confidence and knowledge of God's grace makes you happy, joyful and bold in your relationship to God and all creatures.'
>
> **Martin Luther, from the introduction to the book of Romans, in the German Bible, 1522**

a misguided attempt to merit his favour (thus showing a lack of trust in him), but out of simple gratitude and obedience.

It is tempting to imagine Luther discovering all this in one blinding flash of light. His 'Reformation Breakthrough' has been depicted as being like the conversion of St Paul on the road to Damascus, so that he turned from a medieval theologian to a Protestant reformer overnight. He may even have subconsciously modelled his own account of his 'conversion' on that of St Paul. Yet over these crucial years, it seems that Luther made a number of steady steps forward in crafting this new – or as Luther would have put it, rediscovering this old – theology.

Staupitz's advice, to focus on the cross of Christ and his thought that true penitence begins rather than ends with a sense of God's love for him, seems to have helped. Luther's new understanding of humility and the cross is another step forward. At another point, he seems to have clearly concluded that the common slogan of pastoral advice to 'do what lies within you' was a fundamental mistake. All of these contributed to a gradual change in his theological orientation.

During these years, besides his lecturing, Luther managed to write and publish a short commentary on the *Seven Penitential Psalms*, a group of Psalms regularly used to help penitents prepare for confession. He also wrote an exposition of the Lord's Prayer, and another one on the Ten Commandments, alongside numerous sermons and letters. It seems that Luther wanted to go back to work his way through all the standard Christian texts, reworking them in terms of his developing understanding of Christian theology.

'Hence it is most absurd... to use the commonly accepted statement "God infallibly pours his grace into him who does what is within his power" to mean that he does something or can do something. For as a result of this the whole church has almost been overturned, obviously because of such confidence in this statement.'

Martin Luther, *Commentary on Romans*, summer 1516

Battles in Wittenberg

Meanwhile, things were progressing in an interesting fashion in Wittenberg. As students gossiped excitedly about the content of Luther's lectures, rumours started circulating among the university faculty about this new theology. At the same time, as Luther became increasingly confident that what he had rediscovered was in fundamental conflict with the teaching of many recent theologians, he began to be bolder in pointing out the inadequacies of the theology he had been taught.

Aristotle and medieval theology

Medieval scholastic theology had largely been built using the ideas of the Greek philosopher Aristotle (384–322 BC). Aristotle's works, which had mostly been lost during the early Middle Ages, had been rediscovered in the 11th and 12th centuries through the Christian West's encounters with the Muslim world, which had kept translations of Aristotle in Arabic. Thomas Aquinas and other scholastics had used Aristotle's ideas as a framework for explaining Christian theology.

On 25 September 1516, Bartholomäus Bernhardi, one of Luther's students, was due to be examined. The examination took the form of a disputation, where the student orally defended a number of propositions under cross-questioning from his theological examiners. Under Luther's supervision, Bernhardi wrote a series of propositions, or theses, which basically reproduced what Luther had said in his lectures on the book of Romans. They also heavily criticized the use of Aristotle's theology in scholasticism. Luther's colleague Amsdorf sent the theses back to Erfurt, where they were met with a sharp intake of breath and some displeasure by Trutvetter and Arnoldi, the very people who had taught Luther theology some years before. When the disputation finally took place in Wittenberg it caused a minor stir. A regular meeting of Luther's monastic order in

Heidelberg in May 1518 gave him another chance to try out his new theology on some colleagues. His bold statements such as 'it is not the person who does much who is righteous, but the person who believes much in Christ, without works', and its talk of the need to be a 'theologian of the cross', again raised a great deal of interest.

By this stage, Amsdorf had been won over to Luther's ideas. Others in the Faculty of Theology, for example Lupinus and Karlstadt, were far from happy. Karlstadt rose angrily to refute Luther's view that the Bible and the early Fathers of the church were deeply opposed to scholasticism. Luther encouraged him to go away and read Augustine for himself, in the new original version. During a trip to nearby Leipzig in January 1517, Karlstadt duly bought a copy of Augustine's works. He read them in order to prepare to argue Luther into submission but, to his astonishment, found that Luther was, in fact, right. Augustine's theology and that of the scholastics on these vital questions of God's grace, salvation and justification were like chalk and cheese. Even Petrus Lupinus came over to Luther's side, although he was never quite as enthusiastic as others. By the summer of 1517, the Wittenberg Faculty of Theology was buzzing with these new ideas.

Throughout 1517, Luther was working on a commentary on part of Aristotle's *Physics*. It was heavily critical of the philosopher and the use made of him by scholastic theologians. Luther felt that Aristotle's whole ethical system, with its underlying view that people become good by trying to do good things, started in fundamentally the wrong place – with human works, not God's grace. It was far too superficial – goodness requires a change of heart not just outward behaviour. This commentary never appeared. Instead, it grew into a series of 97 theses or propositions which were to be defended by Franz Günther in the University of Wittenberg in September 1517, in his examination to become Bachelor of Divinity. Luther called this work a *Disputation Against Scholastic Theology*, in which he launched a full attack on Aristotle and on Gabriel Biel's understanding of justification – in fact, on the whole edifice of scholastic theology, whether *via antiqua* or *via moderna*.

This was not an explanation of a new theology, but a final break with the old one. This was Luther throwing down the gauntlet, and the point was not lost back in Erfurt, where his old tutor Trutvetter commented that he no longer considered his old pupil a true logician. This didn't worry Luther unduly – this was still an argument among professors, a storm in an academic teacup. Yet it was not destined to remain this way for long. Two months later in November, Luther was to write another set of theses – 95 of them this time – that were to change his life and the course of history irrevocably.

The Fight

In Wittenberg, life was full. Luther had a full teaching load, working his way through lecture courses on the books of Romans and then Hebrews. Alongside this work, as District Vicar he had to manage several other Augustinian monasteries, a desk groaning with theological texts to be studied, letters to be answered, preaching responsibilities in Wittenberg's city church just off the market square and, of course, the continued daily round of monastic services. Added to all this, Luther was keen to make sweeping changes to the syllabus of the university. He wanted to replace the study of Aristotle and medieval commentaries with courses on the Bible, St Augustine and the other church Fathers. As anyone involved in education knows, changing a curriculum in mid-flow is no easy task, and Luther spent many hours working on it. Outside Wittenberg, however, few people noticed him, and all seemed quiet.

The archbishop

Albrecht of Brandenberg was nothing if not ambitious. In 1513, the cathedral chapter of Magdeburg elected him archbishop. It was not long before he had also become administrator of Halberstadt. Finally, the chapter of Mainz elected him as their new archbishop as well, making him the highest-ranking churchman in the German empire. Holding several such offices at once was, of course, strictly speaking, illegal, but he had found a way of getting round the problem. Pope Leo X had allowed Albrecht to accumulate these offices on condition that he paid a certain fee. The deal was that Fuggers, the great medieval banking house in Augsburg, was to advance the sum of 29,000 gulden to Rome. Meanwhile, Albrecht was to allow the sale of a papal 'indulgence', a certificate of the remission of punishment for sins, in the areas under his ecclesiastical control: Brandenburg, Magdeburg, Halberstadt and Mainz. Half of the proceeds from the sale of the indulgence were to go to repay the debt he owed to Fuggers. The other half was to go directly to Rome. This was a serious matter for this astute church politician. It was vital that the sale went well and so he appointed as his main agent for this enterprise a Dominican friar known as an expert in the field, a man called Johann Tetzel.

From the 13th to the 15th centuries, a number of developments took place in the theory of indulgences. First, they gained a measure of theological rationalization. According to Thomas Aquinas and then the 14th-century theologian Alexander of Hales, Christ and the saints had generated more than enough merit for their own salvation. This 'extra' merit was designated as the 'treasury of the church', a kind of store of merit which could be dispensed to others by the pope, who had inherited the power of the 'keys' of heaven and hell given to St Peter (Matthew 16:19). This was like a very ample spiritual bank account, which could be drawn upon by the pope at any time, and given to those who were worthy of it. Indulgences, therefore, applied the merit of Christ and the saints to Christians who obtained them.

Second, indulgences came to be applied not just to the temporal or earthly punishments imposed by the church, but also to punishments still to be endured in purgatory. In time, indulgences could be obtained not just for the purchaser, but for his or her deceased relations who, it was assumed, were in purgatory, waiting for release.

Third, it became possible to obtain a 'plenary indulgence', in other words, an indulgence which covered all potential satisfactions or punishments demanded by the church. And, finally, by the end of the 15th century, indulgences could be obtained through a gift of money to the church. Before this, indulgences were normally obtained by such spiritual exercises as going on a crusade, seeing a collection of relics or visiting shrines. Now it had become possible, quite simply, to buy indulgences.

The theology of indulgences

Indulgences belonged to the penitential system of the medieval church. When a Christian sinned, he or she would go to a priest to confess. The priest would pronounce the forgiveness of God, and then normally ask for certain 'satisfactions' to be fulfilled – acts which served as 'temporal punishments' (those imposed by the church, not by God) for those sins. Thus, medieval theology made a distinction between 'guilt' and 'punishment'. Only God could forgive guilt – a priest could pronounce remission of guilt, but could not dispense it. Punishment, however, could be imposed by the church and, of course, remitted as well. An indulgence was simply a certificate which allowed some of these 'temporal' satisfactions or punishments to be remitted or reduced.

Albrecht's indulgence

Johann Tetzel was not allowed into Wittenberg, as it was just outside Albrecht's territory, and Frederick the Wise, the Elector of Saxony, jealously guarded the rights to such things in his own regions. However, Tetzel came near enough for some of the townspeople to be tempted over into the nearby villages of Jüterborg and Zerbst, in the region of Brandenburg, to buy Albrecht's indulgence. Luther knew nothing of the political and financial manoeuvring behind this particular indulgence. He did, however, begin to notice Wittenbergers leaving town to hear Tetzel's preaching, and returning with their indulgence certificates. He heard that in some neighbouring towns, regular sermons were being cancelled in order to give room for Tetzel and others to preach the virtue of indulgences. Luther also caught sight of a copy of Albrecht's *Instructio Summaria*, the document which accompanied and explained the indulgence. As he read the document, he was concerned by what he saw. Albrecht's indulgence seemed to make promises far beyond even what was common in the theology of indulgences from the past. Officially, indulgences were only meant to apply to church punishments, not guilt before God. Albrecht's indulgence seemed to promise much more than this – full forgiveness of sins and the remission of all guilt, with its promises of 'the total remission of all sins' for purchasers, and for their relations in purgatory. Or to put it in the most charitable terms, the *Instructio* failed to make it clear that it only applied to satisfactions, not forgiveness.

Luther was very conscious of his position and responsibilities as a Doctor of Theology, a university professor and, hence, a theological guardian of the church. So, especially in the light of his newly developing theology, he felt under compulsion to protest. Sensing he was treading on dangerous ground, and after some anxious hesitation, he wrote another set of theses – 95 this time – which he called a *Disputation on the Power and Efficacy of Indulgences*. On 31 October 1517, he sent these along with a rather timid and respectful letter to Albrecht of Brandenburg himself. On the same day, he wrote along similar lines to his own local bishop, Jerome Schulze in Brandenburg, alerting him to Tetzel's appearance in his diocese. In a later version of the story, told by his subsequent friend and close colleague, Philipp Melanchthon, Luther also raised the issue for academic debate within the university and beyond, by pinning the theses to the door of the castle or university church in Wittenberg, which served as an academic noticeboard.

'Don't you hear the voices of your wailing dead parents and others, who say, "Have mercy on me, because we are in severe punishment and pain. From this you could redeem us with a small alms and yet you do not want to do so..."'

John Tetzel, in an indulgence sermon, c. 1517

The 95 Theses

Reading the theses today often surprises. There is nothing in them about justification by faith, the authority of the Bible, the priesthood of all believers or any of the well-known Reformation doctrines. They look like an academic theological exercise concerning an obscure corner of late-medieval church practice. It is not even as if attacking indulgences was anything new. They were already fairly notorious, and several notable church figures had expressed their doubts about them. Luther's theses hardly seem likely to shake the Western world to its core. They are, in truth, much less radical and shocking than the 97 theses on scholastic theology which Luther had written a year earlier. When he wrote about indulgences, Luther did not dispute their value; he merely protested against the abuse which he perceived in Albrecht's offer. He assumed that if the pope really knew what was going on in this German corner of the Christian world, he would surely want to put a stop to such practices.

From the 95 Theses

Out of love and zeal for truth and the desire to bring it to light, the following theses will be publicly discussed at Wittenberg under the chairmanship of the reverend father Martin Luther, Master of Arts and Sacred Theology and regularly appointed Lecturer on these subjects at that place. He requests that those who cannot be present to debate orally with us will do so by letter.

1. When our Lord and Master Jesus Christ said, 'Repent,' he willed the entire life of believers to be one of repentance…

20. Therefore the pope, when he uses the words 'plenary remission of all penalties', does not actually mean 'all penalties', but only those imposed by himself.

21. Thus those indulgence preachers are in error who say that a man is absolved from every penalty and saved by papal indulgence…

24. For this reason most people are necessarily deceived by that indiscriminate and high-sounding promise of release from penalty…

42. Christians are to be taught that he who sees a needy man and passes him by, yet gives his money for indulgences, does not buy papal indulgence, but God's wrath…

50. Christians are to be taught that if the pope knew the exactions of the indulgence preachers, he would rather that the basilica of St Peter were burnt to ashes than built up with the skin, flesh and bones of his sheep.

Luther's main point was that people were being offered false security. Whatever the intention, the result of such indulgence preaching was to encourage ordinary Christians to trust for their salvation in the power of indulgences, and to lessen the necessity of true repentance. Tetzel's memorable and often-used rhyme, 'as soon as the coin in the moneybox rings, the soul direct from purgatory springs', was denounced as purely a 'human doctrine'. As Luther puts it in thesis number 52: 'It is vain to trust in salvation by indulgence letters, even though the indulgence commissary, or even the pope, were to offer his soul as security.'

Nonetheless, it was this set of theses, not the others, which lit a fuse. And the reason was not so much theological as political. Albrecht of Mainz was too committed financially to take this protest lying down, because the selling of the indulgence was a key part of the deal he had struck to pay his debts. He was no great theologian, more a man of fine taste and elegance, yet when he received Luther's letter, he saw in it a clear threat to his chances of raising the required money to finance his debts. He also saw in it a challenge to his own authority and that of the pope, who after all had expected him to sell the indulgence. This was certainly not Luther's intention. In fact, as he says later, he was concerned at this point to defend the pope, not to attack him, by pointing out a practice which could bring him into disrepute.

The gathering storm

At first, although Luther was well aware that he had taken a bold and dangerous step, nothing happened. He heard nothing from Albrecht, and his own bishop only sent a mild letter of warning about the theses' probable effect. Luther showed the theses to a small circle of his own friends, but even in Wittenberg they did not create much of a stir. When the Elector Frederick had them read to him during a journey, he simply commented gruffly on how 'the pope will not like this'. For the next few weeks, the silence was uncomfortable.

Gradually the theses began to spread. Printers in Leipzig, Nuremberg and Basel published copies which began to circulate widely. Christoph Scheurl, an old friend of Luther at Nuremberg, wrote to an Augustinian friar at Eisleben: 'Pirckheimer, A. Tucher and Wenzeslaus are amazed and delighted with his theses. C. Nutzel translated them into German and I sent them on to Augsburg and Ingolstadt.' By such means, the theses travelled. A trickle of letters began to arrive at the door of the friary at Wittenberg, congratulating Luther on what he had written. However, the theses were not only falling into the hand of friends.

> 'May every single sermon be for ever damned which persuades a person to find security and trust in or through anything whatever except the pure mercy of God, which is Christ.'
>
> Martin Luther, *Explanations of the 95 Theses*, 1518

Albrecht initially asked the University of Mainz for an opinion (which they carefully avoided giving too strongly), and at the same time alerted the pope himself to the matter. When Johann Tetzel saw the theses later in the year, he perceived a similar threat to his livelihood as an indulgence seller. Another Dominican friar from Frankfurt on the River Oder, Conrad Wimpina, who had some old scores to settle with the University of Wittenberg, wrote a set of counter-theses on indulgences, giving no ground at all to Luther's concerns. In March 1518, an opportunistic but foolhardy bookseller from Halle tried to sell a consignment of 800 copies of Wimpina's theses in Wittenberg. Some university students soon swarmed around him and commandeered the remaining copies, which they burned in a great bonfire in the market square.

By now, even though he had still heard nothing formally, Luther was aware of the hornet's nest he had disturbed. He began to worry that, with their widespread appeal, the theses might be misunderstood. A document written in pithy phrases, intended to be supplemented by detailed disputation and argument, was being read out of context and as a full statement of his views. He decided to write another piece, the *Explanations of the 95 Theses*, trying to fill out his position. Again, he insisted that the pope cannot forgive sins – only God can. Indulgences can have no effect at all on souls in purgatory, only on the temporal punishments inflicted by the church in this life. It is not sacraments, but faith in the sacraments, which justifies.

Publication of the *Explanations* was delayed on the advice of Luther's bishop, until later in the year. In the meantime, a sermon of Luther, *On Indulgences and Grace*, appeared, which spread the forest fire yet faster. Tetzel produced more theses, his own this time, flatly contradicting Luther's views. More seriously, a well-known theologian, Johann Eck from Ingolstadt, took issue with Luther. Until this point, Luther had seen him as a friend, but now he came out openly as a firm opponent. This came as something of a shock. To Luther, Tetzel was a silly, irritating trafficker in grace who was out of his depth theologically. Eck, however, was a serious theologian, a man Luther respected, and whom he had expected to share his concerns, coming out on the opposite side. Perhaps this matter would not be sorted out as straightforwardly as he hoped after all.

Responses from Rome

When Albrecht's letter first arrived in Rome, Pope Leo X dismissed the affair as a minor quarrel between a few argumentative German monks, which he could safely delegate to his lesser officials to sort out. As complaints kept arriving, however, the papal court, or curia, decided to deal with Luther once and for all by summoning him to Rome. In the meantime, an elderly commissioner of the Sacred Palace in Rome, Sylvester Mazzolini, known as Prierias, was asked to compose a proper answer to this troublesome friar. He, like Wimpina, Tetzel and Eck, focused on one main issue. The problem was not Luther's views on indulgences; it was his implied attack on the pope.

Such an attack was far from Luther's intention. But intentions and effects are not the same thing. His opponents repeatedly accused him of having opposed the pope's authority by his opposition to indulgences. Luther had attacked not just a few excesses by the indulgence sellers, but he had questioned much of the theological basis on which they (and the pope, who sponsored them) stood. This theology had for centuries given them a validity which the word of an obscure German friar could not contradict.

On 7 August 1518, Prierias's treatise arrived on Luther's desk in Wittenberg. Luther was now formally accused of heresy and summoned to Rome for trial. On the one hand, this development made him even more aware of how perilous his situation was. On the other, he was surprised not so much by Prierias's argument, but by the lack of it. The commissioner simply asserted that neither the pope nor general councils of the church could make mistakes, and that it was impossible, as Luther had done, to draw a distinction between the practice of the church and its teaching. In particular, it genuinely surprised Luther that Prierias, like Wimpina and Eck before him, had singularly declined to argue on the grounds on which Luther had asked to be judged. Luther had asked explicitly to be shown from scripture that he was wrong. The papal theologians replied that the pope and church councils said that he was wrong, and they did not argue from scripture at all. As far as Luther was concerned, they were missing the point.

Although Luther felt strengthened in his opinion by the failure of the theologians to answer him to his satisfaction, at the same time he was worried. Until now, he had thought that scripture, the pope and the church councils were all united against the abuses of the traffic in indulgences. But it was becoming clearer to Luther that he and scripture were on one side, with the pope, the councils and the theologians on the other. The affair did not seem to be going to plan. There was also the worrying business of the summons to Rome. He was meant to be there by 7 October 1518, and Luther knew full well what that meant. To be summoned to Rome and declared a heretic could only mean one thing: a public burning. This was not his main concern; he had counted the possible cost of his actions some while before and, in his most gloomy moments, he had often declared his willingness to be put to death. Foremost in his mind was his desire that his objections be heard fairly, and that the church be rescued from what he increasingly saw as a tyrannical and oppressive regime, which was unwilling to engage in serious theological debate but simply wanted to silence him whatever the cost.

> 'I had so secured and armed my disputation with scripture and papal decretals that I was sure the pope would damn Tetzel and bless me.'
>
> **Martin Luther, 1541**

Some friends suggested to Luther that he should ask to be examined in Germany, rather than in Rome. He wrote to Georg Spalatin, personal secretary to Frederick, the Elector of Saxony, to put the idea to him. Only if Frederick refused to let him travel to Rome could Luther legitimately escape the inevitable and ominous trip to the heart of the papacy.

At the time, an imperial Diet was meeting in Augsburg. This was a business meeting of the Holy Roman Empire, attended by many dignitaries, to sort out a long list of financial, political and religious concerns. The papal representative at the Diet was the smooth, sophisticated and humane Cardinal Cajetan, the Superior General of the Dominican Order. He had arrived in Augsburg with a number of tricky issues on his agenda. First and foremost, there was the matter of the Turks, who were

threatening Christian Europe and had recently approached the
outskirts of Vienna. Cajetan was charged with persuading the
Germans to pay a special tax to fund the defeat of the invaders,
a difficult task, given the level of German dissatisfaction with
the amount of taxation already levied by Rome, and the long-
standing grievance that Rome seemed to have a stranglehold
on most clerical and monastic positions in Germany. Besides
this, the emperor Maximilian was dying, and wanted to
ensure that his grandson Charles had enough votes from the
imperial Electors to succeed him. As Charles was already ruler
of most of Spain, this would have made him a serious rival
to the pope's political aspirations, and so again Cajetan had
to be wary. A minor side issue, which he hoped to get out of
the way relatively easily, concerned an Augustinian friar from
Wittenberg University, who had denounced indulgences.

Cajetan was an able and clever theologian. He had read
Luther's theses and, despite his sympathy with many of them,
still felt that their implicit criticism of the papacy could not
be allowed to stand. He was hoping to resolve it by means of
discussions with Luther's political and ecclesiastical superiors,
Frederick and Johann von Staupitz.

When Frederick and Georg Spalatin arrived to see Cajetan,
they suggested that rather than summoning Luther to Rome,
Cajetan should meet Luther face to face. Keeping in mind
the more important business of the Diet and Frederick's
crucial vote in the forthcoming imperial election, Cajetan
secured agreement from Rome for the plan. Thus, Luther was
summoned to Augsburg.

The hearing at Augsburg

Towards the end of September, even though the Diet had
officially ended, Luther set out on foot for Augsburg. His mood
was sombre, knowing full well the possibility that he might never

see Wittenberg again. During the week-long journey, friends he stayed with warned him of the danger awaiting him. He arrived – tired, nervous and unwell – and, after a day's recovery, he reported to Cajetan for the hearing.

Cajetan initially took a paternal, slightly condescending approach, saying that he did not want an argument, but simply to hear Luther apologize for the disturbance he had caused, and say that he would not cause any further trouble. Luther replied by asking what he had done wrong. Cajetan picked out two of the 95 Theses: number 58, which denied that the merits of Christ were the treasury of the church, and were therefore available to be dispensed as indulgences; and number 7, where Luther's explanation claimed that faith was needed for a proper reception of the sacraments. These, Cajetan confidently asserted, were clearly opposed to previous papal teaching. Luther replied that the papal 'bulls', or decrees, to which his accuser referred, clearly twisted the meaning of scripture, and when it comes to a choice, one should always choose scripture over papal bulls. The argument continued over authority, penance and grace – with no agreement about any of it. After retiring for a day to reconsider, Luther again appeared before Cajetan to profess his loyalty to the pope, and to state that he was unaware of having said anything that was not 'sensible, true and catholic'. On the third day, Luther submitted a written defence of both theses, citing numerous scriptural texts in their support. All of this Cajetan dismissed as 'mere words'. He repeated his demand that Luther recant straightaway or leave.

Luther was on dangerous ground. Cajetan had clearly shown that Luther's views were opposed to papal teaching. Luther could not dispute this, but could only insist that the popes had been wrong, and that it was quite possible for a pope to err. Luther waited to hear from Cajetan. Apart from an unsuccessful attempt to get Staupitz to persuade Luther to recant, nothing came. The days passed, Luther waited and the tension grew. Staupitz, filled with foreboding, absolved Luther

of his monastic vows, to give him the freedom to escape if
it came to that. Luther lodged a formal appeal to the pope
against the way he had been treated, but by this stage he was
edgy, and far from confident. Eventually, sure he was about to
be arrested, Luther was hurriedly smuggled out of Augsburg,
despite the locked city gates, and rode furiously during the
night to Nuremburg. Greatly relieved and exhilarated, he
arrived back in Wittenberg on 31 October 1518, a full year since
the whole business had begun.

Cajetan, meanwhile, wrote to Frederick to demand that
he hand over the heretic friar immediately. This was a crucial
moment in the affair. If Frederick decided to
do so, Luther would surely be condemned and
burned. Yet, either out of fairness to the case or
out of loyalty to the honour of his own university,
Frederick chose to refuse the cardinal's request.
He replied, saying that Luther had still not been
shown where his errors lay according to scripture.
Not for the last time, Luther's political master
came to his defence.

> 'Only faith in the word of
> Christ justifies, makes a
> person alive, worthy
> and well prepared for
> the sacrament.'
>
> **Martin Luther,** *Proceedings at*
> *Augsburg,* **1518**

Debate at Leipzig

Luther's troubles were far from over. Reflecting upon events
at Augsburg, he wrote up an account of the tense days there,
in which he made absolutely clear his rejection of the papal
teachings on indulgences. He expressed the issue which was
increasingly becoming clear to him – that none of his opponents
were willing to argue with him from scripture.

From the end of 1518 and through the following year,
writings both in popular German and academic Latin began to
flow more rapidly from Luther's pen. The failure of Cajetan to
refute or silence him at Augsburg seemed to give him confidence
to speak out more boldly. Pamphlets containing sermons and
treatises on subjects as diverse as penance, baptism, marriage,

prayer and preparing to die emerged from his Wittenberg study. The university was attracting large numbers of students, drawn by Luther's growing notoriety and the excellent teaching of the newly arrived Professor of Greek, Philipp Schwarzerd, who used a Greek form of his name, Melanchthon. In the lecture halls, Luther began to work his way through the book of Galatians, followed by a renewed look at the Psalms. His workload became even heavier as he took his turn as Dean of the Faculty of Theology. The indulgence affair had gone relatively quiet. The matter was left in the hands of Karl von Miltitz, a diplomatic Papal Chamberlain from Saxony, who tried to mediate between Luther and the papacy. Miltitz achieved some success in preventing the matter from blowing up again by persuading Luther to keep quiet, on condition that Luther's opponents did the same.

Things were not destined to stay that way. After Johann Eck's attack in March 1518, Luther had replied privately, not wanting this debate to add to his complications. Eck did not reply, so it seemed that here, too, things had fallen silent. While Luther had been away at the Heidelberg meeting of the Augustinian order, however, his Wittenberg colleague Andreas Karlstadt, feeling that the honour of his colleague and university were at stake, replied to Eck with 380 strongly worded theses of his own. Eck could not ignore these, so he challenged Karlstadt to a debate, which was eventually arranged under the auspices of the University of Leipzig in July 1519. In preparation, Eck produced theses which he would defend, which made it quite clear that it was not Karlstadt he wanted to argue with, but Luther. Even though he would have preferred Karlstadt to keep quiet, Luther was never one to refuse an argument. Now he was fully drawn in and, despite his reassurances to Miltitz, theses and counter-theses passed between Luther and Eck over the spring of 1519. The main issue emerged again as the same one as before – the supremacy and authority of the pope.

> 'He never produced a syllable from the holy scriptures against me.'
>
> **Martin Luther**, *Proceedings at Augsburg*, 1518

Councils and conciliarism

When Pope Gregory XI died in 1378, two rival claimants emerged – one Italian (Urban VI) and one French (Clement VII) – both claiming the title 'Pope'. In 1409, the Council of Pisa disputed the claim of both, and elected a third candidate, Alexander V. This divide, known as the 'Great Schism', lasted until 1417, when the Council of Constance elected Martin V pope. This gave rise to the question of who held final authority in the church: general councils or the pope? Several councils met throughout the 14th and 15th centuries, and 'conciliarism' was the movement which argued that councils, not popes, were the final court of appeal in the church. The 'papalists' generally won the argument, and the failure of conciliarism is often seen as a contributory factor in the success of the Reformation, which promised to bring the changes that many conciliarists had hoped for.

At his desk in the friary in Wittenberg, between giving and working on the publication of his lectures on Galatians, preaching every evening in the city church on the Lord's Prayer and the Ten Commandments, Luther set to work, poring over Canon Law, decrees of church councils and papal decrees. Now he began stating clearly and publicly his belief that the papacy was merely a human institution, that its supremacy over other churches had only been established 400 years ago, and that it had no basis for special divine authority in the holy scriptures. Privately, he went even further. His researches alarmed him, as he wrote to Georg Spalatin in March: 'Confidentially, I do not know whether the pope is the antichrist himself or whether he is his apostle, so miserably is Christ (that is, the truth) corrupted and crucified in the decretals.' Even his friends were becoming nervous.

The Leipzig debate began at the end of June 1519. Eck having arrived two days before, the Wittenberg party arrived en masse, with a rowdy group of armed students in tow. Unlike Augsburg, which was a private hearing, this was a formal, public academic debate, with official judges, namely the theologians and canon lawyers of the universities of Erfurt and Paris. The debate began with Eck and Karlstadt spending seven turgid days debating free will, and arguing over whether Karlstadt was allowed to bring his books to the debating hall to quote from. Then came the main event, the face-to-face encounter between Eck and Luther himself.

To his surprise, Luther found that Eck was not overly concerned with indulgences. Again, the papacy was the sticking point. Eck's case rested on two points: biblical texts which had traditionally been understood to give primacy to Peter and his successors (for example, Matthew 16:18 and Luke 22:32); and a decree of the Council of Constance in 1415. At Constance, the Bohemian Jan Hus had been tried and burned for his heresy in declaring that the papacy had only human, not divine, authority. Eck roundly accused Luther of holding the same view; thus, he should be classed with Hus as a heretic, deserving excommunication and death.

Luther countered Eck with his arguments that the early church had known nothing of papal supremacy, and that Greek Christians had never acknowledged it. Matthew 16 gave the 'keys' of heaven and hell to the whole church, not just to Peter and the bishops of Rome. Yet Luther was being argued into a corner by a skilful opponent. He had to admit that in many respects the Council of Constance had been wrong, and that Hus, the notorious heretic, was in fact right. To say that a truly constituted council of the church could err was indeed a bold step – an important one which made the divergence between Luther and the papacy even sharper, despite Luther's protestations to the contrary.

The debate continued over penance, purgatory and absolution.

Mosellanus on Luther

A contemporary description of Luther comes in an account of the Leipzig debate by Petrus Mosellanus, Greek scholar and humanist from Leipzig University:

Martin is of medium height, with a gaunt body that has been so exhausted by studies and worries that one can almost count the bones under his skin; yet he is manly and vigorous, with a high, clear voice. He is full of learning and has an excellent knowledge of the scriptures... He knows enough Greek and Hebrew to allow him to pass judgments upon interpretations... In his life and behaviour, there is nothing of the stern stoic or grumpy fellow about him... In social gatherings he is gay, witty, lively, ever full of joy... He is sometimes too violent and cutting in his reprimands.

Karlstadt is of shorter stature, with a face dark brown and suntanned, a voice indistinct and unpleasant, and a memory that is weaker, and he is more rapidly aroused to anger.

Eck, in contrast, is a great tall fellow, solidly and robustly built... His mouth and eyes, or rather his whole physiognomy, are such that one would sooner think him a butcher or common soldier than a theologian... he has a phenomenal memory. If he had an equally acute understanding, he would be the image of a perfect man.

Seventeen days after it had begun, the disputation ended, and the Wittenbergers returned home with a decidedly bad taste in their mouths. Luther was upset about his treatment in Leipzig. The townspeople had seemed to treat him as if he had already been declared a heretic. The supposedly neutral Leipzig theologians had seemed to side with Eck from the beginning. And the city council had been unfriendly, only sending to the Wittenberg quarters one crate of wine, compared with the lavish feasting they bestowed on Eck. While Eck was invited to preach all over town, Luther was only allowed one sermon. Eck had argued cleverly but deviously, often conceding points to his opponents, only then to claim that he had brought them round to his own opinion. Both sides claimed victory. The theology faculties charged with deciding on the debate in Erfurt and Paris eventually declined to pass a verdict and, although the universities of Louvain and Cologne predictably came out in favour of Eck and against Luther, formally, the debate ended inconclusively. For Luther, the whole affair 'began badly and ended worse'.

Yet the debate had aligned Luther clearly with a position that was judged heretical. He might have felt that his understanding of scripture had prevailed, but that did not help if the happy agreement between scripture, the church Fathers, the pope and the councils, which he had hoped to demonstrate, lay in tatters. Luther found himself driven more and more onto 'scripture alone' as his foundation. The medieval papacy had seen no essential conflict between church and scripture, even stating, as Prierias had done, that scripture derived its authority from the church, and was therefore subject to the teaching and authority of the contemporary church. Luther also wanted to keep church and scripture together, but when they disagreed, when there was a choice to be made between them, there was no doubt where his trust lay. The word of God, which is found in scripture, with Christ at its centre, was the only ultimate place upon which a person can stake his life. Only there could Luther find a word of God which would prevail against the storms of conscience and conflict. Against this, the church's teaching was merely human and unreliable. Luther and the papacy were now on a collision course.

CHAPTER 5

The Climax

Back in Wittenberg, news arrived that Luther had already been burned in effigy in the streets of Rome. 'It is said that the most severe of all punishments is waiting for me,' he wrote anxiously to Spalatin. His encounter with Eck at Leipzig had renewed his interest in the ideas of Jan Hus, especially after a brief talk with a Bohemian observer at the debate (the church in Bohemia was still influenced by Hus's ideas, and still at loggerheads with the papacy). Luther managed to get hold of a copy of Hus's work on the church, and was amazed to find he agreed with it: 'I have taught and held all the teachings of Jan Hus but thus far did not know it... I am so shocked that I do not know what to think when I see... that the most evident evangelical truth was burned in public and already considered condemned more than 100 years ago.'

Wittenberg was unable to cope with the numbers who wanted to study under Luther, Melanchthon and the rest. Luther's own mood swung violently. At times, the depressions he had suffered in the monastery at Erfurt returned. Letters of this period give brief glimpses into his despair: 'I am terribly busy right now, and at the same time completely overwhelmed by trials,' and, 'My ship is tossed about: sometimes hope, sometimes fear rules.' Yet alongside these episodes of darkness, Luther seemed possessed with an energy beyond his own: 'Who knows whether the Spirit himself is not driving me on with his force, since it is certain that I am not carried away by zeal for fame, money or pleasure.' Writings poured from him, as he grew in his sense of certainty that whatever Cajetan, Eck and an ever-increasing number of theologians wrote against him, he had stumbled upon the truth.

The debate was now shifting towards the sacraments. In the friary and in the churches of Wittenberg, Luther continued to celebrate Mass, to baptize children born to the citizens of the town and to hear confession. At Augsburg, Cajetan had explicitly contradicted his notion that faith is needed for the proper reception of sacraments. The issue had come up in Leipzig with Eck. At the same time, Luther was increasingly finding in the sacraments a steady rock on which to stand when troubled by inner turmoil.

The doctrine of transubstatiation had led to an almost magical reverence for the elements of bread and wine in the late-medieval church. On many occasions, the Mass came to be observed as a spectacle rather than partaken of, as people watched the miracle of God appearing before their very eyes. By the beginning of the 14th century, it was common for the laity to be given the bread alone, to prevent the possibility of sacrilege by accidentally spilling the true blood of Christ. The same Council of Constance which condemned Hus in 1415 also formalized this into the official practice of the church. Masses were said as a form of prayer – for the soul of one who had died, for a safe journey, a good harvest or good weather. It was an act of supplication to God, something offered to him, in return for which he was expected to give a reward. The traffic in Masses for the dead had reached such proportions that the church was barely imaginable without it. Wills left complex financial arrangements for priests to say Masses for the soul of the departed, chantry chapels were built or added to churches specifically for the saying of Masses for the dead, and brotherhoods were founded to celebrate and provide for Masses to be said for their members.

Luther on the Mass

From late 1519 into the next year, Luther returned to the theme in sermons, letters, and treatises such as *The Holy and Blessed Sacrament of Baptism* (November 1519), *A Treatise on the New Testament, that is the Holy Mass* (July 1520) and *The Babylonian Captivity of the Church* (October 1520). For Luther, sacraments were simply 'promises which have signs attached to them'. Any sacrament had two parts: a visible sign (such as water, or bread and wine) and a word of promise. As Augustine had indicated centuries before, a sacrament was a kind of embodied, visible word.

Transubstantiation and the Mass in medieval life

The doctrine of transubstantiation, officially adopted by the church in the fourth Lateran Council of 1215, uses Aristotle's distinction between the 'substance' of a thing, its inner reality or essence, and its 'accidents', or outward appearance and quality. When a priest says the words of consecration over the bread and wine at the eucharist, although the accidents remain the same (it still looks, feels and tastes like bread and wine), their substance is actually transformed into the body and blood of Christ. This is then offered to God as a sacrifice for sin.

From this early stage, Luther insisted that the Mass could in no sense be offered to God as a form of prayer, a plea for mercy or a good work which earned merit. It was, instead, a simple sign of God's word of forgiveness offered in the gospel. 'The Mass,' he wrote, 'is the promise of Christ.' At its very heart are the words of Christ: 'This is my body given for you.' The direction of the event is thus radically reversed – it is not an offering from us to God; it is a promise or pledge from God to us. And if it is essentially a promise, the only valid response can be to trust that the promise is true – in other words, faith. The focus of the event is likewise shifted, away from the one performing the service – the priest, often alone, whispering the words to himself, as Luther himself had done in the friary at Erfurt – to the one receiving the bread and wine in simple trust. A Mass can therefore only benefit the one receiving it; it cannot be said for anyone else. For Luther, the whole industry of Masses for the dead was a complete waste of time and money. The Mass also had an important communal aspect. It was a sign of belonging to Christ and his saints, assuring the believer of membership of God's holy people. It was a sure pledge that Christ and his people stand with you.

Luther was becoming bolder with every step. In October 1520, his publication *On the Babylonian Captivity of the Church* went further still. Thanks to the controversies of the past three years, he now saw that indulgences were not only abused, but were 'wicked devices of the flatterers of Rome'. While at Leipzig he had maintained that the papacy still had human, if not divine, authority, now he denied even this, saying plainly that he considered the pope's rule over the church to be tyrannical, anti-Christian and evil.

> 'Certain people... have rashly dared to assert that the Christian people ought to receive the holy sacrament of the eucharist under the forms of both bread and wine.'
>
> **Decrees of the Council of Constance, June 1415**

Bearing in mind his understanding of the Mass as primarily a representation of the promise of God in Christ, which binds the community together, Luther objects in the strongest terms to three elements of medieval sacramental practice and theology. First, the denial of the cup to the laity is a scandal, an example of the clergy's tyranny over ordinary laypeople. The Mass belongs to the whole community, not just the priest. Second, transubstantiation, while not wholly wrong, is an unnecessary complication and is downright misleading if it encourages a magical understanding of the rite. It is not to be found in scripture, and the church certainly should not have condemned those who did not believe it, such as Wyclif or Hus. Worst of all is the idea that the Mass is some kind of 'good work' or 'sacrifice'. The Mass is a promise to be believed, not a work to be performed. Christ comes to us as a gift from God, not a demand. This is the source of the endless merchandising of grace, the commodifying of religion which has led to the widespread, corrupt and abusive trade in Masses.

Baptism, likewise, is a promise to be believed. It is not baptism itself that saves, but faith in the promise which baptism conveys. 'There is no greater comfort on earth than baptism,' declares Luther. For Luther, baptism stands over and against his experience of sinfulness and despair, telling him that God has forgiven him from sin, and one day will free him from sin altogether. Penance, or private confession to another Christian (it does not have to be a priest) is a good thing – yet the sinner must despair of the attempt to achieve a perfect contrition or even attrition for sin. What matters is hearing and trusting God's promise of forgiveness. Luther went so far as to say that if a priest were absent, any Christian, even a child or a woman, could pronounce absolution – and if the promise was believed, it would still be effective! The other four sacraments of the medieval church – confirmation, marriage, ordination and extreme unction (the last rites) – do not fit into Luther's definition of a sacrament, as they possess no visible sign ordained by Christ to go along with the word of promise.

To prepare to receive the sacrament, it is pointless to try to generate a perfect sorrow for sins. It is pointless in fact to try to bring anything of one's own to the sacrament. All that is needed is a simple trust that God keeps his promises. Here is a strong sacramentalism, much stronger than in many versions of later Protestantism, yet with a radical shift away from the standard sacramental teaching of the church, both at the levels of theology and practice. If this were taken seriously, almost the entire understanding of priesthood and church life would need to be changed. Luther knew that he was being provocative: 'I am uttering unheard of and startling things, but if you will consider what the Mass is, you will realize that I have spoken the truth.'

'For God does not deal, nor has he ever dealt with man otherwise than through a word of promise... We in turn cannot deal with God otherwise than through faith in the word of his promise.'

Martin Luther, *On the Babylonian Captivity of the Church,* **1520**

In June 1520, another attack from Prierias arrived, which only confirmed Luther's conclusion that the papacy was not interested in reform. He began to conceive the idea of a 'manifesto' laying out his demands – not so much the theory, but the practical changes he wanted to see introduced. While the *Babylonian Captivity* was composed in Latin – a treatise intended for an educated, scholarly audience – Luther now decided to appeal publicly, in German, for all to read. If the pope or the bishops would not carry out reform, then it was the task of the secular leaders to do so. Like many others, Luther had high hopes for the new young emperor, Charles V, who, despite Cajetan's efforts, had now been elected emperor in succession to Maximilian I. Luther had also received unexpected support from among the German nobility, for example the knights Ulrich von Hutten and Franz von Sickingen, who represented a humanistic form of German nationalism. They were not especially interested in Luther's theology, just keen to back anyone furthering the claims of Germany against the predators of Rome.

> 'Whoever does not hold to the teaching of the Roman Church and the pope as an infallible rule of faith, from which even holy scripture draws its power and authority, is a heretic.'
>
> Sylvester Prierias, *Dialogue Against the Arrogant Theses of Martin Luther on the Power of the Pope*, 1518

The resulting treatise, *To the Christian Nobility of the German Nation*, addressed directly to the new emperor, was a rampaging, sometimes intemperate, but gripping description of what Martin Luther considered to be wrong with the church. The 'Romanists' had cleverly built a threefold structure around themselves, which rendered them impervious to criticism from any quarter. Lay critics of the church were never taken seriously because of the supposed priority of the clergy (the 'spiritual estate') over the laity (the 'temporal estate'). The scriptures could not critique the church either, because the pope was the only one allowed to interpret them. To cap it all, church councils were powerless, because only a pope could call a council. The result, wrote Luther, was an unaccountable institution which had placed itself above censure, and which had lost all likeness to the suffering, crucified Christ through its fondness for wealth, political influence and power.

In countering these three notions, Luther was at his most potent. At the heart of his argument was the vision of a more egalitarian, communal understanding of the church, where each member could play an active and decisive part. The distinction between clergy and laity was merely one of function and role, not priority. Baptized laypeople, such as the emperor, or the knights to whom he was appealing, had just as much right and responsibility to reform the church as the clergy, especially when the latter would not act. The title 'priest' truly belonged to all believers, because priests were made by baptism not by ordination. Similarly, every Christian, not just the pope, had the duty to read and interpret scripture, to 'espouse the cause of the faith, to understand and defend it, to denounce every error'. The idea that only the pope could call a council had no basis in scripture; when the church was in dire need, it was the responsibility of the lay powers that existed to call the communal voice of the church to speak in a general council. After all, the greatest council of all, the famous Council of Nicea in AD 325, was called not by the pope, but by a layman, the first Christian emperor, Constantine himself!

'Arise O Lord, judge thy cause... Now a wild boar from the forest threatens to ravage the vineyard.'

Pope Leo X, *Exsurge Domine*, 15 June 1520

Luther then rattled off a whole series of demands, 27 in total. They ranged over matters administrative (reducing the number of cardinals and the size of the papal curia in Rome), economic (a fierce critique of Fuggers and the practice of usury), nationalist (German churchmen should appoint German clergy, and German affairs should be determined by German courts), political (the papacy should give up all claim to territorial control or power), clerical (all begging monks should be outlawed, shrines for pilgrimages demolished and Masses for the dead banned) and educational (Aristotle, Lombard and the study of canon law should be banned from the universities and, in theology at least, should be replaced by a simpler study of the Bible and just a few good books of theology). The list was breathless, sweeping and outrageous. Once more, Luther made even his supporters cower when they read it. One of his closest friends, the Erfurt Professor whom he had known as a fellow-monk in the monastery, Johann Lang, tried to persuade Luther not to publish. Too late – it was already being devoured across Germany and beyond within a few days of publication. In Luther's mind now, Rome was not part of the solution, it was the nub of the problem.

Luther's excommunication

To Luther's disappointment, the secular rulers admired what he had written, but did nothing. In Rome, however, it was different. Eck was on the warpath, urging action against the Saxon heretic and volunteering to hunt him out himself. Within Luther's own Augustinian order, voices were heard suggesting that because Luther was bringing them shame and trouble, Staupitz should keep him quiet. Since Augsburg, Staupitz had distanced himself from his younger colleague, much to Luther's dismay. He no longer had any power to make a difference. With the emperor question settled, Rome had no need to keep Frederick the Wise happy. Eck and a number of Italian cardinals worked on the draft of a 'bull', condemning Luther and threatening him with excommunication if he did not recant. It was delivered to a hunting lodge at Magliana, where Pope Leo X was hunting wild boar, at the beginning of May 1520. The final version was dated 15 June, and appeared on 24 July.

Luther was given 60 days to submit. The bull began by likening Luther to the wild boar so keenly hunted by the pope, wrecking the ordered vineyard of God's church. It proceeded to list 41 of Luther's statements, mainly on the sacraments, penitential practice and the authority of the papacy, which were pronounced heretical. If Luther recanted, then his books would be burned, but he would be given a safe conduct to Rome, should

he choose to deliver the recantation in person. If he did not, he
was to be treated as a barren heretic, cast out from the church,
to be delivered to Rome for sentencing.

Eck was charged with responsibility for publishing the bull
in Saxony. This was not too hard a task in Albertine Saxony,
where the Catholic Duke George was in charge. However, it was
a different prospect in the other half, Ernestine Saxony, the
territory of George's cousin Frederick the Wise. Opinion had
turned so far in Luther's favour that Eck was hounded from
town to town as he tried to publicize the bull. Even in Leipzig,
the scene of his 'triumph' just a year or so before,
students jeered at him in the streets, and when
threatening letters arrived at his lodgings, Eck
decided to take refuge in the town's Dominican
monastery. He did not dare to visit Wittenberg. In
Erfurt, a copy of the bull was torn up and thrown
by some students into the slow waters of the River
Gera. Elsewhere in Europe, the bull did not fare
much better.

'The soul... is justified
by faith alone and not
any works.'

Martin Luther, *On the
Freedom of a Christian,* **1520**

Luther became aware of the publication of the bull in July
1520. Meanwhile, feverish attempts were still being made to
stem the inevitable. Miltitz, conferring with Staupitz and other
members of Luther's order, persuaded Luther to write to the
pope in calmer terms, to appeal one last time for a hearing by
the pope himself. In October, Luther composed a letter, trying to
distinguish the pope's person from his office, appealing to Leo
as 'a lamb among wolves' in Rome and laying all the blame for
the affair on 'godless flatterers' such as Eck. It was a last, vain,
poignant attempt to prevent the catastrophe. He attached to it
a work which Luther described as 'a small book... containing
the whole of Christian life in a brief form, provided you grasp
its meaning.'

In it, he wrote of the incomparable benefits of faith. Faith
'justifies, frees and saves'. It gives God the honour he deserves

by taking him at his word. Most strikingly, it joins the believer and Christ as intimately as a husband is joined to his wife in marriage. All of our sin is taken over by him; his goodness and purity become ours. Faith is no mere academic assent to abstract doctrinal truths; it is a personal bond of trust. Likewise, justification is not a cold, objective transaction but a living, warm and mysterious union between ordinary human beings and Christ, their loving redeemer. This work, *On the Freedom of a Christian*, remains one of the most positive and clearest summaries of Luther's teaching on faith and the Christian life, a strange pool of liberty and serenity among the stormy waters of this tumultuous year.

The bull, however, was a different matter. This was the final straw that severed any remaining attachment Luther felt to Rome. At the same time as the rich, warm *On the Freedom of a Christian* came the violent, angry *Against the Accursed Bull of Antichrist* in November 1520. When news of the official burnings of Luther's books at Cologne and Mainz reached Wittenberg, plans began to be hatched for a similar event – but with a very different meaning.

On the morning of 10 December, exactly 60 days after the issuing of the bull, the day on which Luther's period of grace elapsed, Melanchthon invited anyone in Wittenberg University who was concerned for the truth of the gospel to meet at the Chapel of the Holy Cross just outside the eastern Elster gate, a few yards away from the Augustinian friary. Johann Agricola, a supporter of Luther who taught in the Faculty of Arts and in the Faculty of Theology, organized a collection of copies of Canon Law, a standard confessional manual, and some works by Eck and Emser (another of Luther's adversaries) – all of which were thrown onto a bonfire. Eventually, Luther himself emerged from the crowd, carrying a copy of the papal bull, *Exsurge Domine*. Somewhat agitated and clearly tense, with a few quietly spoken words, Luther threw the bull onto the fire. He and the other professors returned through the gate into the city, while the students carried on rowdily, adding other books and pamphlets during the remainder of the day. Now there was no other option but for Luther to be declared an outlawed heretic.

The bull finally excommunicating Luther, *Decet Romanum* was issued on 3 January 1521. Frederick the Wise and Ulrich von Hutten were also mentioned by name as those who had incited Luther in his heresy. When he received the bull, Frederick returned it indignantly, claiming no responsibility for Luther's teaching, and repeating his belief that Luther had still not been properly refuted. Rome backed down and the final version, issued in May 1521 had no mention of Frederick's name or Hutten's, only Luther's.

Luther and the emperor

If Luther had come to the end of the line with the pope, there was of course still the emperor. An imperial Diet had already been planned to begin in January, to mark the beginning of the new emperor's rule. It would be held in the city of Worms, due to an outbreak of the plague in the more traditional location, Nuremberg. The Diet already had a crowded agenda, demanding attention to matters of public order, foreign policy, defence and economic problems. The Luther case was initially not up for discussion but, after the inflammatory events of December, there was no way the Diet could avoid the issue.

Aleander, the papal nuncio, was hoping that the emperor would simply endorse the papal excommunication and impose an imperial ban on Luther, in order to close the matter without any further appeal, or, at the very most, after a private hearing. Frederick the Wise was arguing for Luther to be given a fair and impartial hearing before the emperor and a learned panel capable of judging such matters. Popular support was clearly on Luther and Frederick's side.

Eventually, after a great deal of negotiation and argument, a compromise solution was reached. Luther was to be summoned under a guarantee of safe passage to Worms, but not for a debate. He was to be asked to recant those things he had written against the traditional faith. Even if he did not recant, the leaders of the German estates asked that the complaints against Rome, which Luther had listed in *On the Babylonian Captivity of the Church*, should be looked into. As usual, Frederick had got his way. On 6 March, the call to Worms was issued and, just before Easter, the imperial herald arrived at Wittenberg with the official summons.

All this time, Luther had kept in touch with affairs through Georg Spalatin. He confessed to being 'carried away and tossed about by the waves', but saw in the scriptures the reassurance that God's cause is always opposed and God's truth remains like a rock amongst the storms. He knew that things were looking grim: 'Up to now, one has only played around in this case; now something serious is at hand,' he confided in a letter to Staupitz. He knew that his own death was a very probable outcome of this whole affair.

> 'All of Germany is in an utter uproar; nine-tenths of the people are shouting: 'Luther!' and the other tenth – if Luther is of no consequence to them – at least have "Death to the Roman Court!" as their slogan.'
>
> **Aleander, papal nuncio, at the Diet of Worms, 1521**

Having completed the Easter services in Wittenberg, Luther set out for Worms in a cart and horses provided by the town, with a small party of friends and supporters, including his university colleague, Nicholas Amsdorf, and Jerome Schurff, a local lawyer. The party was led by the imperial herald, and set off towards Leipzig. It was an eventful journey. As the group approached Erfurt, despite Luther's fears about his reputation there, a large welcome party came out to meet him, speeches were made in his honour and he was invited to preach to a packed church. Eisenach, Luther's hometown, welcomed him like a hero, as he preached in the church where he had once sang as a choirboy. After Eisenach, Luther fell seriously ill – whether through travel sickness or nerves it is hard to tell. He arrived in Worms to huge interest from the townspeople on 16 April 1521. The city was heaving with visitors, due to the Diet, and it seemed that everyone wanted to see the famous monk who had turned the world upside down. The tension could be felt in the air.

Immediately, a whole string of 'counts, barons, gilded knights and nobles, both ecclesiastical and lay' came to pay their respects. The day after his arrival, Luther was officially summoned by the Master of the Imperial Cavalry to present himself before the emperor, electors, princes, dukes and all the imperial estates at four o'clock. Luther duly arrived, having to creep through the side streets to avoid the crush of people wanting to see him. He was ushered into a room in the bishop's house next to the cathedral. The scene focused on Charles V himself, seated in the centre. Around the room stood a large gathering of electoral princes, electors and dukes. Frederick the Wise was there – this was in fact the only time he ever set eyes on Luther in person. On a table lay a pile of books. The overcrowded room was hot, with the warm spring weather. Luther, clothed in his usual Augustinian habit, with his wide monastic tonsure freshly shaved, was asked two questions: whether he acknowledged that the books listed under his name and displayed on the table were in fact his, and whether he was prepared to retract anything in them.

To the first of these, Luther's answer was straightforward, if his voice was a little trembling and quiet. Yes, they were his. Whether because he was surprised not to be presented with a list of statements to retract, and instead had been asked to deny whole books, or maybe simply out of anxiety, Luther asked for time to consider his answer to the second question. After some discussion, the princes and the emperor pointed out that Luther had surely had time to think of his answer before he came, yet, out of a desire that things should not be done unfairly, they were willing to give him a day. The hearing was adjourned with a distinct sense of anticlimax.

Overnight and the next morning, many friends visited Luther's lodgings, exhorting him to stand firm. In a brief letter written that evening, he indicated his determination not to give in: 'With Christ's help, however, I shall not in all eternity recant the least particle.'

Late the next afternoon, Luther was conducted back again to the imperial court. The Archbishop of Trier's secretary, Johann Eck (not to be confused with the other Eck, whom Luther had encountered at Leipzig), now asked him for his final answer. The reply, given first in German then in Latin was longer than expected. Luther divided his writings into three: those which were uncontroversial; those written against the papacy, which he could not retract without giving support to papal tyranny; and those written against certain individual defenders of the papacy, which while sometimes expressed too violently, he could not retract either. After all, had not the papacy clearly deceived the faithful by its teaching, and (with a glance at the princes gathered around the room) had it not devoured the property and possessions of the German lands?

Eck told him to get to the point. Did he, or did he not retract his teaching? Then Luther uttered his famous words:

Unless I am convinced by the testimony of the scriptures, or by clear reason (for I do not trust in either the pope or in councils alone, since it is well known that they have often erred and contradicted themselves), I am bound by the scriptures I have quoted and my conscience is captive to the word of God. I cannot and I will not retract anything, since it is neither safe nor right to go against conscience.

After a brief discussion, Eck touched on the thing the church feared most: if it was admitted that Councils contradicted scripture 'we will have nothing in Christianity that is certain or decided.' After a little more discussion, as darkness was beginning to fall, the hearing was concluded in some confusion. Luther left, clearly with a great sense of relief. Some asked if he was being arrested (an assurance was given that he was not); another group of Spanish observers shouted abuse at him.

The next day, the emperor gave his verdict. Conscious of his forebears and the long tradition of Catholic faith in which he stood, it was impossible that a single monk could be right and the whole of the Catholic Church be wrong. Charles was 'determined to proceed against him as a notorious heretic', and expected Luther's political masters to do the same. The following days saw further meetings in which princes and church dignitaries tried to impress on Luther the importance of laws and structure, and to submit his doctrines to the judgment of the imperial court. This Luther was unprepared to do, unless they would make their judgment according to scripture alone. Finally, on 25 April 1521, Eck returned to Luther's lodgings to inform him that he had 21 days in which to return to Wittenberg. He was told that he was not to preach or stir up the people in any way, and that he was soon to be under the imperial ban. The Edict of Worms, Charles's official verdict banning Luther, appeared later in May, and Luther's expulsion became final and public.

Luther had come to Worms expecting, as he put it later, that 'bishops and doctors would fully investigate me there'. Instead of a rigorous theological examination, however, he simply faced a demand to recant. Essentially, Luther was condemned at Worms because he disagreed with the Council of Constance on the nature of the church and the authority of the papacy. Here was an ecumenical council of the church which had spoken quite clearly, yet Luther was utterly convinced that it had been wrong and un-Christian, and that it had condemned the gospel itself. The chief argument used against Luther was that of private judgment. As Eck put it: 'Do not claim for yourself that you... are the one and only man who has knowledge of the Bible, who has the true understanding of holy scripture, to which understanding

'In Antwerp, Luther's writings are being printed in Spanish... In Ghent, the Augustinians proclaim Luther's gospel in all the streets as being the teaching of St Paul, yes, even of Christ... No one knows a way of confronting this heresy; even those who fear Luther speak in his favour.'

Report of the papal nuncio from the Diet of Worms, 1521

the most holy doctors toiling night and day in the exposition of scripture, have attained through great labour and effort.'

Luther at Worms has been seen as the archetypal man against the machine, or the prisoner of conscience. Despite his language, it is clear that the ultimate standpoint to which he appealed was not reason or conscience, but to the manifest teaching of the Bible. What he did took courage, mixed with a certain amount of bravado. It was a reminder to an unwieldy and overblown organization of its need to return to its true identity and to allow itself to be redefined by its foundational charter documents, to be true to itself, and not to allow itself to be shaped by other values and priorities.

Pope and emperor had spoken, and Luther was now an outlaw. For some years, his friends had debated what Luther should do if this were to happen. Some thought he should head for Bohemia or Denmark; most thought he would be banished. Frederick the Wise, the wily politician as ever, not wanting the star of his university to be harmed, yet not wanting to draw the wrath of the emperor, approved a secret plan which was explained to Luther the night before he left Worms. Luther was to go into hiding.

On the return journey, Luther gave notice that he had no intention of abiding by the forthcoming edict, by preaching to great acclaim in both Hersfeld and Eisenach. The imperial herald was sent home, no longer needed, and most of Luther's travelling companions were sent on ahead, on the pretext that Luther wanted to visit relations in nearby Möhra. The next day, as the small party negotiated a valley near Altenstein, a mysterious band of horsemen emerged from the trees. Luther's two remaining colleagues ran off. Luther himself was dragged along on foot for a short distance, then hauled onto a horse and led blindfold on a circuitous route to shake off all possible pursuers. At about 11 o'clock at night, disorientated and exhausted, he finally arrived at an isolated castle fortress known as the Wartburg, on a hilly outcrop near Eisenach. There, accompanied only by the castle watchman and the watchman's family, he was to stay. Apart from a close circle of intimates, including Frederick, Spalatin and a few others who were in on the plan, no one in Europe knew where he was. Many thought he had been killed. At last, after the storms and turmoil of the past four years and the past few weeks, there was silence. No lectures, no hearings, no services, no people – just the strange stillness of the deep forest and the mountain winds.

CHAPTER 6

The Leader

The Wartburg is a lonely place, built along a thin, rocky ridge at the top of one of the densely wooded hills in the Thuringian lands near Eisenach. As Luther was hurried over the drawbridge into his new home, clutching copies of the Hebrew Old Testament and the Greek New Testament, which he had managed to grab as he hurriedly left the cart, his world changed instantly. For a while, the silence seemed like a delicious relief after the turmoil of recent events. During the first two weeks, Luther grew out his monastic tonsure, allowed a thick beard to grow and, for the first time since student days in Erfurt, began to wear ordinary clothes. When visitors came or deliveries were made, all they saw was a strange knight staying in the castle, 'Junker Georg' – in reality the infamous Martin Luther in disguise.

This was all new to Luther. From the cloak-and-dagger antics of the arrest, to the company of his courteous but distant host, Hans von Berlepsch, and the endless hours of enforced idleness, he felt in a different world from any he had known before. He even went on a two-day hunting expedition, the brutality of which he clearly did not enjoy. Soon, Luther was bored and lonely. He thrived on conflict and controversy, and was itching for the battle again. He also yearned for his friends and colleagues at Wittenberg, and before long the letters began to flow. He wrote gossipy letters to Melanchthon and new wife, wanting to know the news from Wittenberg, and reassuring them that they would all be fine without him. He wrote to the congregation in Wittenberg, explaining what had happened, so they did not feel he had abandoned them. He wrote to the knight von Sickingen, who had offered him haven before Worms, dedicating to him a sermon on confession. He wrote to Spalatin, Bucer, Amsdorf and a host of others.

He was plagued by an old enemy – constipation – and gave graphic accounts of his discomfort: 'My stools are so hard that I am forced to press with all my strength, even to the point of perspiration.' He tried pills, and 'had some relief and opened my bowels without blood or force, but the wound of the previous rupture isn't healed yet.'

Melanchthon wrote wistful letters praising Luther's courage and faith. Luther felt the truth was very different: 'I sit here like a fool and hardened in leisure, pray little… yet burn in a big fire of my untamed body. I am ardent in lust, laziness, leisure and sleepiness' and 'The troubles of my soul have not yet ceased and the former weakness of the spirit and faith persists.' A priest came often to offer Mass in the castle chapel, but this did not help Luther much, as the priest tended only to say private Masses, a practice that Luther now believed was a travesty of the real thing. Isolation did not sit well with an extrovert such as Luther, and he experienced his old *Anfechtungen* – doubts, temptations and despair over his sins, against which he would place in the balance again and again the scriptures, his baptism and Christ.

> 'God, if Luther is dead, who will from now on present the gospel to us so clearly? O God, to think of what he might have been able to write for us in another 10 or 20 years!'
>
> **Albrecht Dürer (1471–1528), on hearing a report of Luther's disappearance, 1521**

The struggle with the papacy now having reached a kind of conclusion, Luther's mind turned to the next stage. Now came the tasks of rooting the message in the ordinary people of Germany, helping those who had supported his protest to understand the gospel better, and making the liberating message of faith more widely available and more easily grasped. At Worms, Luther had spoken about a kind of 'reformation' of the church which he wanted to see. Now he had to make this a popular and populist movement.

Writing from the Wartburg

Luther's literary output continued, even from this isolated castle. He wrote a treatise which condemned monastic vows as encouraging an attempt to please God by a monk's own holiness, thus imposing hopelessly unrealistic demands and burdening consciences. He composed guides to help preachers expound the Gospel readings for Advent and Christmas. The renewed study of biblical texts took him even further. With some encouragement from Melanchthon, Luther began to translate the New Testament into German. This, of course, had been done before. Since the invention of moveable type with Gutenberg's press in Mainz in about 1450, printing copies of the Bible had become dramatically easier and cheaper. Various translations in German had appeared before the turn of the century, but these were translated from the official Latin Bible of the medieval church, the *Vulgate*, and so they were translations of translations. They also stuck very close to the original Latin translation, so any mistakes in the Latin were transmitted to the German.

> 'One-third of all books sold in Germany in the early 1520s were by Martin Luther.'
>
> **Stephen Ozment,**
> *Protestants*, 1992

The Greek New Testament which Luther had used in the Wartburg was Erasmus's 1516 edition, published at Froben's press in Basel. Luther now set about translating this into German. Not only was this the first time that the Greek had been used for a full German translation, entirely ignoring the *Vulgate*, but Luther also tried to make it readable by peasants, farmers and miners. 'You have to ask the housewife, the children in the street and the ordinary man at the market, see how they respond, and then translate accordingly.' The result was colourful, vigorous and occasionally funny. In 11 weeks of feverish work, he produced a first draft. It was to be intensely revised by colleagues back in Wittenberg, but it never lost its vivid Luther style, full of imaginative word pictures and earthy language. This draft was the first step towards Luther's famous

German Bible, which did so much to form a clear, independent, modern German language for the coming centuries.

Wartburg and Wittenberg

Naturally, Luther was keen to know what was happening back in Wittenberg. In October 1521, the Augustinian monks in Luther's friary stopped celebrating Mass there. Thirteen monks had left the friary, following Andreas Karlstadt's urging. Some had proposed that all Masses be abolished, and Karlstadt had begun to question the presence of images and statues in the town churches. Visiting monks were being jeered at in the streets, and even the prior of the Augustinian friary was worried about appearing in public, for fear of attack by unruly students.

At this point, Luther's curiosity got the better of him. In December he borrowed a horse, rode through the wintry landscape to Wittenberg, still in his knightly disguise, and arrived at Amsdorf's house. His friends were delighted; after all, this was the first time most of them had seen him since he had left for Worms. They quickly but secretly gathered, urged him not to go near the friary, and briefed him on developments. Luther was upset that many of his writings had still not been published – he suspected that Spalatin had held onto them for fear of inciting further unrest. For his anxious caution, Spalatin received a sharp letter of rebuke. In general, Luther was pleasantly surprised. Reforms seemed to be going well. They just needed a stronger type of preaching to help them along and to curb excesses. Less welcome were rumours he heard, during his secret journey, of violence and rebellion being promoted by some of the peasants in the name of his reforming programme. On his return to the Wartburg, he quickly wrote *A Sincere Admonition by Martin Luther to All Christians to Guard Against Insurrection and Rebellion*. His position was clear: 'No insurrection is ever right, no matter how right the cause it seeks to promote.' Here was an important step towards Luther's political theology, which was to develop over the coming few years.

Back in the Wartburg, Luther heard that three men from the nearby town of Zwickau had turned up at the gates of Wittenberg, claiming direct visions and revelations from God. Luther was not overly concerned at first, but when Melanchthon wrote of them in awed tones he began to take them seriously. Claims of direct revelation from God should be taken with a pinch of salt, Luther stated. Were they called? God usually calls people either through the church or through special signs and wonders – just saying that God has called you proves nothing.

Also, have they experienced spiritual distress, *Anfechtungen*? The sign of someone having spoken directly with God is usually that they are terrified, not serene! Luther's theology of the cross was still alive and well: 'Do not listen if they speak of the glorified Jesus, unless you have first heard of the crucified Jesus.'

The three prophets had also, for the first time in this whole business, questioned whether infants should be baptized. Luther had been expecting this issue to come up. He gave his arguments – there was no reason to doubt that God can give faith to infants even from the very start of life, and on that basis they should be baptized, as the whole church had always maintained. Now some different notes were sounding in the Luther affair. The trouble was coming not from the right but from the left. It was a signal that from now on much of Luther's energy was to be spent fighting battles within the ranks of those wanting reform of the church, rather than outside them. Now, the struggle was with those who wanted to change too much rather than too little, who wanted a Reformation which looked rather different from the one Luther had in mind.

'Everyone should arm themselves and attack the priests in their fat nests... Like magicians they dress up in silk and velvet of all colours, make gestures like monkeys when they take the bread and wine... You can receive the forgiveness of sins without all this nonsense... The external audible word of the priest is not God's word but their own.'

Nicholas Storch, one of the Zwickau prophets, in a sermon, c. 1521

On Christmas Day, wearing ordinary clothes, Karlstadt gave

both bread and wine to laypeople during communion in the
parish church, just metres away from his own house. He began
to speak like the men from Zwickau, saying that God spoke
directly to the heart, not through books, even the Bible. In
January, a document called the *Wittenberg Ordinance* appeared,
originating from Karlstadt. It said that, henceforth, both bread
and the cup were always to be given to the laity in communion,
and were to be taken into their hands, not just placed on the
tongue. The central part of the service was to be said in German,
not Latin, the bread was not to be elevated and the language of
sacrifice was to be dropped from the liturgy. All images were to
be removed, and private Masses and brotherhoods banned from
the town. After all, were not these precisely the reforms which
Luther had urged to take place?

The town was restless. Students had interrupted sermons,
loudly disrupted a Mass being said in the parish church and
chased the priests away from the altar. In another attack, a
group incited by Karlstadt's teaching had torn down most of the
statues, images and altars in the city church, leaving it in chaos.
A letter came from the citizens of Wittenberg, asking Luther to
return. Luther now believed that: 'Satan has intruded into my
fold at Wittenberg.' The Zwickau prophets were out of control,
and Luther was fearful of a general revolt in the surrounding
countryside. All of this could threaten the delicate balances of
the reforming movement and alienate important supporters,
such as Frederick the Wise. While always affectionate towards
his friend, Luther was unhappy with Melanchthon's timidity:
'He gives in too easily to his moods, and bears the cross more
impatiently than is fitting for a disciple,' Luther wrote to
Spalatin. Melanchthon's letters always seemed to be anxious,
looking for guidance – he was not fitted for the role of overall
leader, and he needed Luther's strength. This was not the time
for idleness so, against Frederick's advice, in March 1522, Luther
left the Wartburg for the last time, to return to Wittenberg.

Luther's return

Luther arrived on 7 March, a Friday. On Sunday, clothed again in monastic garb, he climbed into the pulpit of the city church, with a packed and expectant crowd listening for his first words. The atmosphere was electric, and the opening equally dramatic: 'The summons of death comes to us all, and no one can die for another. Every one must fight his own battle with death by himself alone.' Here again was the characteristic search for a theology which would stand the test in the day of trial. Wittenbergers had learned the central importance of faith in the Christian life. Now they needed to learn the importance of love. Faith, love and freedom. For eight days, Luther preached on these same themes each day to students, faculty and anyone who could get away from their work to listen.

A Christian must know that 'his whole life and being is faith and love. Faith is directed towards God, and love towards man and one's neighbour.' The basic theme was that they were doing the right things in the wrong way. Yes, private Masses should be abolished – yet change must be effected by God's word, not by compulsion. God's word must first create understanding minds and willing hearts; then change can be introduced. If change is brought in too early, as Karlstadt had done, it only creates bad consciences, actions forced out of people, not done gladly – a mockery of true religion, which must come from the heart. 'We must first win the hearts of the people... when you have won the heart, you have won the man.' Luther's own experience over the past five years was the prime example. All he had done was to preach and write about God's word, and sit in Wittenberg drinking beer with his friends. He had passed no laws and

'Therefore, all those have erred who have helped and consented to abolish the Mass... You say that it was right according to the scriptures. I agree, but what becomes of order? For it was done in wantonness, with no regard for proper order and offence to your neighbour. If beforehand, you had called upon God in earnest prayer, and had obtained the aid of the authorities, one could be certain that it had come from God.'

Martin Luther, in a sermon preached at Wittenberg, 9 March 1522

forced no consciences, and the papacy had been dealt a far more

grievous blow than any army could have given it. The last thing Luther wanted was the replacement of a Catholic legalism with a new evangelical legalism.

These sermons changed everything. Soon known as the 'Invocavit Sermons' from the name of the Sunday on which they began, they were a remarkable demonstration both of Luther's rhetoric and also his immense personal authority in Wittenberg. All the reforms from the *Wittenberg Ordinance* were turned back. This was the beginning of the end of Karlstadt's time in Wittenberg. He was aggrieved that his programme had been defeated, and that many of the townspeople who had enthusiastically supported his radical agenda, including his colleague Zwilling, now admitted they had gone too far. Karlstadt began to loosen his ties with the town, buying a farm and seeking to live a peasant lifestyle there (although still drawing a salary, much to his colleagues' disgust!). Soon, he left the town altogether. He became vicar of the small town of Orlamünde, renounced his academic titles, refused to wear robes and continued to preach his egalitarian, spiritualistic style of faith to anyone who would hear. He and Luther were to meet again in 1524 while Luther was engaged in a preaching tour of the area. They engaged in a heated argument in the Black Bear Inn at Jena, where they parted even further apart than ever.

'It is not good enough to serve for nothing and do good to the neighbour as Christ did and Dr Luther says... We must, above all else, be like Christ in our inner being and have the likeness of Christ. These are higher and more essential articles than to love the neighbour.'

Andreas Karlstadt on Martin Luther, 1525

Luther's position in Wittenberg seemed unassailable. However, quelling the Wittenberg disturbances was by no means the end of the story. Further afield, when others heard what had happened, many were shocked that Luther had failed to carry through the consequences of what he had started. The rumblings against Luther in the reforming camp were getting louder.

One of the most strident voices against Luther came from Allstedt, near Eisleben. Thomas Müntzer had studied at Leipzig, Frankfurt an der Oder and briefly at Wittenberg itself. He later took up a preaching position in Zwickau. After a spell in Prague, he was appointed preacher at Allstedt in 1522, and quickly became a popular and controversial figure. At one time he had been a follower of Luther, by whom he said he had been 'brought to birth by the gospel'. Yet it was not long before he turned against his former teacher. Like Karlstadt, Müntzer tended to a much more 'spiritualist' understanding of Christianity, learned from his reading of Tauler and the German mystical tradition, which Luther himself had flirted with in his early years. Already by 1521, Müntzer was writing of 'mere scripture', which was all he heard from the priests. Instead, he wrote, God's word had to be heard directly from God's mouth: 'Anyone who does not feel the Spirit of Christ within him or is not quite sure of having it, is not a member of Christ, but of the devil.' Luther and Melanchthon worshipped a 'dumb God', one who did not speak to the soul, but only through dead words on a page. For Müntzer, a spiritualized, inner-directed faith was allied to a politically charged programme. The blame for Germany's woes lay at the feet of the princes and the priests who had oppressed the 'common man'. This, for Müntzer, included both the peasants themselves and the merchants, whose cause Müntzer tended to espouse, in contradiction to Luther, who saw them as greedy parasites.

> 'Our beloved Martin acts ignorantly because he does not want to offend the little ones... But the tribulation of Christians is already at the door... leave your dallying, the time has come!'
>
> **Thomas Müntzer to Melanchthon, 1522**

In 1524, Müntzer's opposition to Luther became public and bitter, as he launched a full-scale attack on what he saw as Luther's cowardice, compromise and unwillingness to bear the suffering which the gospel demanded. The piece, unsubtly introduced as *A Highly Provoked Vindication and a Refutation of the Unspiritual Soft-living Flesh in Wittenberg whose Robbery and Distortion of Scripture has so Grievously Polluted our Wretched Christian Church*, was a vitriolic and furious essay, outdoing even Luther at his most abusive.

Luther's political theology

Müntzer's attack was directed at a theology of government which Luther had begun to develop since the Wittenberg unrest some years before. Those events had made Luther reflect not just on theological matters of faith and works, but also on the down-to-earth question of how the gospel related to social and political realities. In February 1522, Duke George, ruler of Albertine Saxony, a papal loyalist and one of Luther's severest opponents, banned the sale of Luther's German Bible in his own lands. What were Luther's supporters to do there? Should they obey? Did George have the right to make such an edict?

In an important treatise of 1523, called *Temporal Authority: To what Extent should it be Obeyed?*, Luther divided the world into two 'kingdoms'. In the 'kingdom of God' are the righteous – those who trust in Christ and who obey the civil law gladly from the heart. In the 'kingdom of the world' lie the unrighteous, those who do not obey the civil law gladly, and who need to be restrained for the good of society and social order. Because there are these two kingdoms or realms, God rules the world in two different ways. He governs the righteous – who produce good works naturally, and have no need for laws or compulsion – with the word of the gospel. He governs the unrighteous, however, by the punitive power of secular government. Reluctant to obey, the unrighteous need the compulsion of laws, punishment and courts, and all the paraphernalia of the legal system. If the

> 'Sleep softly, dear flesh! I would prefer to smell you roasting in your own arrogance in a pot or cauldron by the fire, smitten by God's wrath, and then stewing in your own juice.'
>
> **Thomas Müntzer to Martin Luther, 1524**

world were full of true Christians there would be no need for law or a penal code – like a tree producing good fruit, obedience to God's law would emerge automatically. Because the world was not like this (Luther thought that true Christians were few and far between), there was a need for the sword, or secular government, to enforce obedience and punish disobedience.

It is vital not to confuse these two. The world cannot be ruled by the gospel, which advises Christians to turn the other cheek, to forgive repeatedly and so on. These instructions only apply in the kingdom of God. Conversely, Christians cannot be ruled by external laws. The gospel cannot be imposed by coercion because faith is a matter of freedom, not force. A Christian therefore acts in two different spheres. When acting in a *public* role on behalf of others (for example, as a magistrate or soldier), then he must act according to the kingdom of the world: wrongs must be punished, the law enforced and justice enacted. When acting in a *private* capacity, where it is a matter of offences against himself, wrongs must be forgiven, and injustice simply endured and suffered. The result of all this is that, while secular government is a necessary part of God's government on the world, there are clear limits to its jurisdiction. The Duke Georges of this world had no right to ban the sale of Luther's Bible, as this was a clear case of temporal (political) government interfering in a matter of faith – a confusion of the two kinds of government.

The peasants' revolt

This political theology became controversial as events progressed over the next few years. The rumours which Luther had heard during his brief secret journey to Wittenberg from the Wartburg had a measure of truth. Complaints from peasants against their rulers were nothing new, yet in the 1520s, a slowly but surely growing chorus of protest began to be heard. For decades now, as medieval cities grew in

population and influence, as political power became more
decentralized into the hands of local princes and territorial
estates, the rural peasants began to lag well behind – especially
in the more industrialized areas. Local rulers were introducing
new regulations and curtailing the ancient rights of village
communities. This was a society in transition, and the losers
began to make their voices heard. This time, however, there
was a new note in the tune. In Luther's gospel, especially what
he had written in *To the Christian Nobility* they heard many of
their demands spoken of as part of a reformation of the church
according to scripture.

Not surprisingly, many disenfranchised people
saw in Luther's ideas a rallying cry to the kind
of social justice they had long sought. Over the
following years, pamphlets were printed, speeches
were made and sermons preached which echoed
these demands. In February 1525, a follower of
Luther called Christoph Schappeler, and Sebastian
Lotzer, a furrier, drafted *The Twelve Articles of the
Peasants*. This became a standard and widely used
statement of the peasants' demands. These clearly
echoed Luther's earlier calls. The first article
asked for the right for a community to elect its
own pastor, rather than having him imposed upon
them by a distant bishop or by the pope. Such a
pastor should 'teach us the holy gospel pure and
simple, without any human addition, doctrine or ordinance...
since the scripture clearly teaches that only through true faith
can we come to God.' The articles continue with demands such
as the abolition of compulsory tithes, the end to serfdom, rights
to fish, hunt and collect wood on lands appropriated by the
nobles, and an end to burdensome taxation. The document ends,
reminiscent of Luther at Worms, with a pledge to withdraw any
of these articles if they are shown to be 'against the will of God
by a clear explanation of the scripture'.

'The righteous man of
his own accord does
all and more that the
law demands. The
unrighteous do nothing
that the law demands;
therefore they need the
law to instruct, constrain
and compel them to
do good.'

Martin Luther, *Temporal
Authority: To what Extent
Should it be Obeyed?*, **1523**

With scriptural references liberally sprinkled in the margins, the *Twelve Articles* were both moderate and evangelical. They uttered no threats of violence, just the refusal to pay unjust taxes. The authors explicitly denied the accusation of insurrection and insubordination. What is more, they clearly breathed good Wittenberg air. Luther's appeal to scripture and his appeal for reform of the church and social life find an echo in this carefully worded and peaceable text.

When Luther read the *Twelve Articles* in April 1525, he responded in a friendly but firm manner, in his *Admonition to Peace: A Reply to the Twelve Articles of the Peasants in Swabia*. In terms of pure justice, Luther was clearly on the side of the peasants. The demands of the *Twelve Articles* were 'right and just'. To the nobles, his words were blunt: 'It is not the peasants who are opposing you, it is God himself.'

Luther's tactics, however, had not changed from his battles with the unrest at Wittenberg a few years before. The pamphlet sounded a dire warning that the protest must not become violent. Force or bloodshed can never be justified in the cause of the gospel, and those who live by the sword will die by the sword. Luther tried to wean them away from unnamed preachers (though he clearly had Müntzer in mind), who were trying to urge them to armed uprising. Luther could foresee only damage and disaster to both sides, and to Germany as a whole, in the way things were going. Luther's motives for all of this were complex. Paul taught in Romans 13 that God institutes political authorities, and their injustice is no excuse to rise up against them. Luther advocated a kind of non-violent protest, in which the Christians' weapons are prayer, preaching and suffering the consequences. Hidden somewhere in all this was also a fear for the cause of reform if it got caught up in a doomed peasant rebellion which alienated the very princes

> 'All who believe in this Christ become loving, peaceful, patient and agreeable. This is the basis of all these articles of the peasants...
> and they are basically concerned with hearing the word of God and living according to it.'
>
> **Schappeler and Lotzer, *The Twelve Articles*, 1525**

from whom Luther expected so much. Alongside this lay a deep-seated medieval fear of anarchy and disorder, which made Luther unable to see any justification for rebellion.

Luther's words, while firm, were still fairly moderate, and had no effect whatsoever. So far, the peasants' protest had been for the most part peaceful – basically consisting of large carnival-type gatherings where grievances were aired, demands read out and speakers cheered heartily, until they moved on to another town to gather more support. Now, as the summer months approached, the revolt took a more violent turn. Among many others, the cities of Erfurt and Salzungen fell to the rebel 'armies'. On a visit to Eisleben to establish a new Christian school there, Luther heard first-hand stories of bands of peasants roaming the countryside and attacking castles, monasteries and towns. He even found himself heckled as he preached – something he was not used to experiencing in Wittenberg. Luther was shocked. He now thought that events were well out of his control – or anyone's. On his return journey, repenting of his earlier gently reasoned tone, he composed what was to become one of the most notorious of his writings, *Against the Robbing and Murdering Hordes of Peasants*. This short piece, just a few pages long and intended as an appendix to the *Admonition to Peace*, concerning the extreme wing of the rebellion, urged the authorities to put down the revolutionaries with as much aggression as was required: 'This is the time of the sword, not the day of grace.'

'We have no one to thank for this disastrous rebellion, except you princes and lords... As temporal rulers, you do nothing but cheat and rob the people so that you may live a life of luxury and extravagance. The poor common people cannot bear it any longer.'

Martin Luther, *Admonition to Peace*, 1525

Luther's fire was particularly directed at Müntzer, who was by now installed as leader of the rebel-controlled town of Mühlhausen. The 'peasants' had started a rebellion and, by plundering property and killing people, deserved death. Even worse, they had done this under the banner of the gospel as self-styled 'Christian brethren'. Rulers would be quite justified in punishing the rebels without trial, although they should, by rights, offer them a chance to repent. Luther saw the rebellion as a kind of disease, which had to be eradicated through a policy of slaughter of anyone infected or liable to be infected – he even advocated no mercy for hangers-on to the movement, as well as active participants in violence.

'The German peasants' war'?

Although this is a popular term for the uprisings in central Europe from 1524 to 1526, it is seriously inaccurate. First, it was not really 'German' (events occurred outside Germany, and there was no particularly 'German' consciousness behind it). Second, there were many non-peasants involved (anyone who felt left out of the changing shape of society was attracted to the movement, including miners, townspeople who had no vote and merchants who felt that their rights were being curtailed by the political estates). Finally, only the last phase, lasting a few months, could be called a 'war' – most of the protests were deliberately non-violent and peaceful.

A week later, the rising came to a swift and bloody end near Frankenhausen in Thuringia. The peasant armies in Thuringia and Saxony had come together in a mass gathering near the town. Urged on by Müntzer, who assured them that God would protect them from the bullets of their enemies, they went into battle against the far superior military forces of the princes of Hesse, Brunswick and Saxony, who had joined forces to crush the revolt. The result of the battle was a foregone conclusion. The princes' guns began firing into the peasant ranks. As the first casualties fell, and the awful realization dawned that God would not protect them from fire, the rebel army panicked. They tried to run back into the town – and were mown down by the princes' troops. Müntzer was captured inside the city walls, then tortured and executed, along with about 50 other rebel leaders. This was only one of several battles fought in different parts of Europe as the revolt was put down, but it was the most catastrophic for those involved – and also for Luther's reputation. His 'harsh letter' appeared just as news was spreading of the Frankenhausen disaster, and it seemed as if Luther was directly responsible. Moreover, read out of the context of the tumultuous and confused events of May 1525 (several printers published it quite separately, as a free-standing tract) Luther appeared to be justifying senseless murder and indiscriminate state violence.

Assessing Luther's politics

Luther's political ideas do require some assessment. Luther's 'Two Kingdoms doctrine', as it became known much later, was originally an argument about liberty and toleration of religious freedom – there are areas of conscience which politics cannot touch. Much of the original treatise, *On Temporal Authority*, concerns the limits of political power (due to the immediate context of Duke George's attempt to ban Luther's Bible) rather than the other side of the equation, the limits of relevance of the gospel in secular life. However, it is easy to see how this kind of political theology could result in the advice Luther gave to the princes in the revolt of 1525. At its best, this doctrine was a valid attempt to separate out two spheres which had become confused. In a world where the papacy and local bishops claimed political and territorial power, and where secular rulers were tempted to interfere in matters of faith, Luther wanted to insist that it was the task of rulers to rule and clergy to preach. Both are agents of God's rule, both are demonstrations of God's care for his world – but the two must not get confused.

'Therefore let everyone who can, smite, slay, and stab, secretly or openly, remembering that nothing can be more poisonous, hurtful or devilish than a rebel. It is just as one must kill a mad dog; if you do not strike him, he will strike you, and a whole land with you.'

Martin Luther, *Against the Robbing and Murdering Hordes of Peasants*, May 1525

At its worst, the doctrine gave the impression that the gospel had no relevance at all to secular life, and was only of significance for some inner, private sphere. Luther's language was often confused and imprecise, and he left many questions unanswered. For example, are Christians subject to the law of the land or not? How do you reconcile his call in *Appeal to the Christian Nobility* of 1520 for a secular reform of the church with this later demand for rulers to 'keep their fingers out of the pie'? Later on, Lutheranism was often imposed by the ruler of a region, and Luther would defend this by saying that rulers had a responsibility to legislate on 'externals', defending the state religion. But who is to say what is 'external' and what is 'internal'? In the 20th century, the doctrine was blamed for the German churches' inability (with some notable exceptions) to stand up to Hitler in the 1930s – believing, after Luther, that the church must not interfere with secular government. Perhaps the doctrine was too unclear and too subtle to have much immediate influence. An argument about religious liberty became used as a total political theology, a burden it was not well equipped to bear. However, it is a severe irony that Luther, the ultimate rebel against abusive authority, should have bequeathed a legacy of political conformity.

Whatever we think about the theology, Luther's judgment was politically astute. If he had supported the peasants, then no doubt his cause would have fallen with theirs at Frankenhausen. As it was, he survived – but he lost a good deal of popular support through his stand over the

'God be praised, there is peace in and around the city of Zwickau. Doctor Martin has fallen into great disfavour with the common people, alike with both learned and unlearned; his writing is regarded as having been too fickle.'

Hermann Mühlpfort, mayor of Zwickau, writing after the defeat of the peasants, June 1525

'After this rebellious war was repressed... There was a great and lasting rise in the prices in all things, especially meat. This was followed by pestilence... Evangelical teaching and preaching were accused... of being... rebellious.'

Valerius Anshelm, *Report of Aftermath of Peasants' War*, 1525

peasants' revolt. Opinion amongst the veterans of the rebellion, and those who wanted to see widespread change in church and society, felt that Luther was no longer with them. The Reformation began to go its own way.

CHAPTER 7

The Breach

In the middle of all this, Luther got married. When he had taken his vows in Erfurt, first as a monk and then as a priest, he had doubly bound himself to a life of celibacy. But since then, everything had changed. Still, this was a development neither he nor anyone could have expected even a few years beforehand, especially now, while the peasants' revolt was raging.

In previous writings, Luther had taken an unromantic and practical view of marriage. It was God's designated way of expressing sexual desire and bringing up children. In stark contrast, however, to most medieval Christian teaching, Luther extolled the virtues of marriage over the celibate life. While recognizing that the duties of family life as a noble and godly vocation can change the married person's perspective and lift the spirit above the troubles which marriage often brings, his own mind was not fixed on matrimony. Any day, the imperial authorities might turn up to arrest him; death was still not an unlikely outcome. Marriage was a good thing, but not for him. Not yet, anyway.

Several of Luther's friends and colleagues had already married, including Melanchthon, Agricola and Karlstadt. From the Wartburg, Luther had joked in a letter that Melanchthon would never succeed in fixing him up with a wife. Now, the friary at Wittenberg seemed strangely empty. Most of the monks had left, leaving only Luther, his servant, a former student called Seeberger, and the prior, Eberhard Brisger. No communal meals, no services in the choir, and just the mess of a large house seldom cleaned or cared for. In 1523 a group of nine ex-nuns who had escaped from a Cistercian convent in Nimbschen, near Grimma, arrived in Wittenberg. Because they were penniless, the only solution was to find them husbands – a task Luther undertook with some vigour. Before long, there was only one left, Katharine, or Katie, von Bora – a not unattractive and strong-willed woman of 26, who was by now lodging and helping out along the main street from the Augustinian friary, at the house of Wittenberg's famous painter, Lucas Cranach.

Luther had already been urged to marry by several friends. A letter written in April 1525 contains playful banter about Spalatin's marriage prospects, and the warning that Luther himself might even beat him into matrimony. While on the ill-fated trip to Eisleben, during which he was so disturbed by evidence of the rioting peasants, Luther visited his parents in Mansfeld, who repeated their original hopes that he would get married and give them grandchildren. This seems to have tipped the scales. On 4 May, in a letter to Johann Rühel, an old Wittenberg friend, he writes of how, because of the crisis of the times, he expects death to come sooner rather than later. Nevertheless, he intends to marry before it comes, 'to spite the devil'. On his return to Wittenberg, while setting about to write his 'harsh letter' about the peasants, he also found time to ask Katie, the remaining nun, to marry him.

> 'God has willed and brought about this step. For I feel neither passionate love nor burning for my spouse, but I cherish her.'
>
> **Martin Luther to Amsdorf, just after his marriage, June 1525**

They moved fast. On 13 June 1525 they were officially engaged. The marriage ceremony, conducted by Bugenhagen the town priest, followed – unusually – straight afterwards. The wedding took place in the friary – because Luther did not believe that marriage was a sacrament, it needed no service in church. It was a small affair, involving just Bugenhagen, Justus Jonas, a lawyer called John Apel and the Cranachs. The couple postponed the marriage feast for a fortnight, in order to give time to invite Luther's parents and friends who lived further away.

The timing was certainly strange. Frederick the Wise was dying, the peasants were out of control – and here was Luther, getting married! Most of his friends were dismayed. Melanchthon was angry. He could see nothing but evil rumours and disrepute coming from the haste and the inappropriateness of the timing. His unease might also, in some measure, be explained as pique at having only found out about it after the event. Rumours quickly spread that they had married hurriedly because Katie was pregnant, but she clearly was not, and Luther laughed off all criticism. He undertook the marriage out of typical bravado. By now, what others thought of him mattered little. This was a public display of his freedom from all vows and human regulations; it was finally practising what he was preaching, and a means of silencing 'the evil mouths which are so used to complaining about me'.

Marriage changed Luther's home life drastically, and he soon discovered the delights of friendship and companionship which his earlier treatments of marriage lacked. However, it left a bad taste in the mouths of many who did not know Luther's inner motives. While peasants were dying in the fields of Frankenhausen, Luther it seemed had been thinking only of his own happiness. For many, it cemented a growing rift – but Luther did not care. From 1525 until the end of the decade, Luther found himself acknowledged as the noble instigator of a great change. But he was increasingly isolated, as yawning gaps developed between him and significant reforming groups whose agenda were very different from those preached in the churches and lecture halls of Wittenberg. After the peasants, next came the great humanist, Erasmus himself.

Luther and the humanists

In chapter 2, we looked at the influence of humanism on Luther's early career. Although the Reformation was triggered by Luther, the way it turned out is unthinkable without the influence of Renaissance humanism. Humanists had published original texts of the Fathers and the New Testament, and they had already attacked both scholastic theology and Roman corruption. Nationalistic German humanism, in particular, represented in the past by such writers as Rudolf Agricola and Conrad Celtis, wanted to reclaim Germany's place as a dignified and ancient nation with its own independent language, free from the constraints of Rome and Latin. Luther consciously played to this gallery as he pushed forward his reform proposals for a vernacular, locally controlled church, unencumbered by the burden of Roman theology and taxation.

In Wittenberg itself, the university was seen as a centre of humanism, with its stress upon biblical languages, and its disdain for scholasticism, Aristotle and Lombard. The faculty included notable humanist teachers, such as Christoph Scheurl, who taught law, and who had gained his doctorate at Bologna in Italy. Philipp Melanchthon was appointed Professor of Greek as a humanist scholar – as nephew of the famous German humanist and Hebraist Johannes Reuchlin, what else could he be? As Luther arrived in the university he was involved in a revision of the syllabus, which looked to all concerned like a typical shift in a more humanist direction.

'Erasmus was far from the knowledge of grace, since in all his writings he is not concerned for the cross, but for peace. He thinks that everything should be discussed and handled in a civil manner and with a certain benevolent kindness.'

Martin Luther to Spalatin, from the Wartburg, 9 September 1521

Yet, despite all this, a deep gulf lay between Luther's central concerns and those in humanist circles. As far back as 1516, and again at the Wartburg, Luther suspected that one day he would come to blows with Erasmus. Initial contact between Luther and Erasmus had been relatively friendly, if guarded. Erasmus had tried to ensure a fair hearing for Luther's reforming agenda. As Luther became the notorious heretic of the early 1520s, the Dutchman came under pressure from his compatriot, the new pope Adrian VI, to write openly against Luther. By now, Erasmus's feelings towards Luther were that of an increasingly exasperated parent towards a reckless child. Luther had made his protest, yet now he seemed to be wildly lashing out at everything in terms which were never cool and urbane like Erasmus's own, but tempestuous and wild. Temperamentally, they were like chalk and cheese. Erasmus wanted the debate about reform to be carried on in a civilized fashion, like a polite chat in a university senior common room. Luther's language seemed more at home in bar-room brawls. He was rude, crude and stubborn, needlessly offensive and divisive. Erasmus's main problem with Luther was not so much his doctrine, but his style – or, indeed, lack of it. As Luther made more and more enemies, Erasmus was concerned that he himself would be tarred with the same brush.

> 'Luther is piling on both liberal studies and myself a massive load of unpopularity... Oh, if that man had only left things alone, or made his attempt more cautiously and in moderation!'
>
> **Desiderius Erasmus, letter to Nicholas Bérault, February 1521**

Eventually, Erasmus decided to write about an issue on which he felt Luther really had gone too far. The topic was originally suggested to him by the English king, Henry VIII. In Luther's desire to make salvation dependent solely upon God and not upon any human works, he had claimed that since Adam's fall, free will was an empty illusion. The human will was entirely bound, being unable to choose between good or evil. This position was close to that argued by the great St Augustine back in the fifth century. In March 1524, Erasmus sent to Henry VIII an advance copy of a *Diatribe on Free Will*, which was finally published in September 1524.

Here, Erasmus deliberately took on Luther over a central point of his theology. Erasmus's view of Christianity was fairly simple. In the scriptures, we are urged to turn away from sin and evil to Christ and all that is good, though the outcome was to be attributed to God's grace. Erasmus was prepared to credit human will with some limited capacity to turn to God or to choose not to. More technical questions about whether people can contribute anything to salvation, whether the will is entirely or only partially bound, are uncertain in the scriptures, and should be left to the theologians. At least, they should not become the cause of dissension and division in the church. Luther had even implied that everything was predetermined, and that humans had no choice at all. For Erasmus, this took away any incentive for good action, and led to moral laziness. Basically, we have the capacity to choose whether or not to turn toward the things which lead to salvation, and it is up to us to use that power.

Despite its conscious rejection of Luther, this was a moderate and irenic piece. Erasmus did not write with fury, nor with a wish to stir up trouble. He only took issue with Luther 'reluctantly'. Yet if he hoped that his compromise position would bring harmony, he had reckoned neither with Luther's deepening convictions, nor with the radical nature of Luther's theological position. In December 1524, after the furore over the peasants' revolt had died down, Luther replied with a work which expressed its disagreement even in the title, *On the Bondage of the Will.*

Whereas one of Erasmus's main goals was the avoidance of conflict, Luther delighted in it. The preaching of the gospel always creates opposition, and conflict should not surprise us; in fact, we should expect it. In Luther's eyes, Erasmus is more concerned with peace and quiet than with the truth of the gospel and the glory of Christ. Will no one make any moral effort if we have no power to obey scriptural commands? Good, says Luther – the whole point of God's work in us is precisely to stop us trying to earn divine credit by moral effort and, instead, to throw ourselves on God's mercy. The law is preached not to urge us to good behaviour, but to show us our need for God's grace. It tells us what we ought to do, not what we can do. Scriptural commands are there to bring us face to face with our inability to keep them, so that we will despair of our attempts to please God

> 'If anyone may devise "implications" and "figures" in scripture at his own pleasure, what will all scripture be but a reed shaken with the wind, and a sort of chameleon? There would then be no article of faith about which anything could be settled and proved for certain.'
>
> **Martin Luther, *The Bondage of the Will*, 1525**

by our works, and simply trust in Christ. We have some element of free will in relation to the ordinary choices of daily life, things 'below us' as Luther puts it. But when it comes to things 'above us', questions of justification and our relationship with God, then we have no freedom to act or contribute anything. It is only when God acts upon us, leading to despair of our own resources, that we can begin to become those who do good, arising out of simple faith in Christ.

What particularly annoyed Luther was Erasmus's claim that scripture was not entirely clear on these points. For Luther, the clarity of scripture was a fundamental assumption, especially on this crucial question of justification. The central place of faith, not works, was unequivocal and plain, and left no room for doubt. If God's promise on this count is dubious or unclear, then it brings the whole question of salvation into doubt. It would plunge sinners such as Luther back into the anxious uncertainty from which he felt he had been so joyfully liberated. Again, Luther's test of the interpretation of scripture lies in the terrors of conscience. Erasmus's casual resort to a lack of clarity in scripture on this vital question is no help when the conscience is plagued with doubt and fear. What is needed is the solid rock of a word from God which cannot be doubted, not the unsteady vagueness of an ambiguous interpretation.

For Luther, Erasmus's apparently innocuous admission of a small limited part to be played by human free will gave the game away. If this were true, then the whole of salvation came into doubt. If any part of salvation rested upon an effort of the human will, then Luther was back where he started – with his fears about whether he had ever done enough to merit grace. Only if salvation was all the gift of God, simply accepted by faith, could it bring joy and certainty – because then it rested upon the firm and reliable promise of God, not the uncertain and unreliable actions of men. In Luther's view, the conclusion was plain – without grace, the will is not free to choose good: 'Man without grace can will nothing but evil.'

Luther made assertions; Erasmus made tentative surmises.

Luther thundered; Erasmus reasoned. The two could not be more different. At least Luther credits Erasmus with having located the real issue. He had not focused upon more trivial points such as indulgences, the papacy and purgatory: 'You and you alone have seen the hinge upon which all turns, and aimed for the vital spot.'

The aftermath

All over Europe, educated people read these two treatises, fascinated by this heated argument between the two most famous scholars of the day. Luther argued passionately, perceptively and not always fairly. He accused Erasmus of frivolity, being effectively a godless sceptic. This was not exactly fair to Erasmus's concern for the church and his desire for peaceful evolutionary change. Luther also flirted with some dangerous ideas in this work. In discussing predestination, he posed a contrast between God revealed and God hidden. This went much further than his previous ideas on this subject, even going so far as to suggest that there is a hidden dark side to God that we cannot know, that is not revealed to us, which wills the death of sinners who are not part of God's elect. Some of Luther's friends were uncomfortable with this, as well as with his strong words about Erasmus and the insistence that the will is entirely chained. Melanchthon, in particular, quietly distanced himself from Luther and, over the coming years, developed a position much closer to Erasmus's than Luther's, though not identical with it.

> 'Erasmus... exposed the appealing alliance of Renaissance and Reformation as only a temporary coalition.'
>
> **Heiko Oberman, *Luther: Man Between God and the Devil*, 1989**

Erasmus, who was more than a little vain and sensitive to criticism, was hurt and stung by Luther's criticisms and dismissive tone. He eventually wrote a pained reply, which Luther, at the time plagued with bad health, evidently did not read until much later. When angry, Luther could be intolerant, being quite unwilling to see any other point of view but his own. He could make things worse by exaggerated polemic, which made more enemies than friends. He possessed a clarity of mind and an emotionally involved theology which had helped him grasp the sharp point at which the church had taken a fatal turn away from the doctrine of God's grace. These same characteristics also made it hard for him to compromise and to see things from standpoints other than his own.

The controversy with Erasmus did not mark a fundamental break between the Reformation and humanism – humanist methods were still welcome in Wittenberg, and even more so in Swiss reforming circles. Luther himself continued as the leader of a widespread movement, while Erasmus was never quite at home either in evangelical or papal circles. The controversy did, however, alienate a number of potential supporters, put off by Luther's resort to attack on someone who, after all, shared much with him in his desire for a purer, simpler church, with a higher regard for the scriptures, and cleansed of the abuse of generations.

Luther's capacity to make enemies out of friends was confirmed even more as the decade drew to a close, as the European evangelical movement itself split apart over the interpretation of the sacraments. Here, too, differences in style between the ex-scholastic Luther and the more humanist-educated Swiss reformers lay hidden behind the debate, to which we now turn.

The controversy over the eucharist

Marburg Castle is an imposing place, perched high above the city in the central German region of Hesse. Today, it still draws the eye and dominates the skyline, peering down on the fertile surrounding countryside. In the 16th century, Marburg was a fair-sized city in the territory ruled over by the Landgrave Philip of Hesse, its houses, churches and inns clustered tightly around the hill on which the castle stood. It was here, in 1529, that one of the most significant conversations took place in the history of the Reformation. It was one which had fateful consequences for the future of the movement, and which has left its mark on the European religious and political landscape ever since.

Luther's early writing on the eucharist was aimed primarily at the abuse of the Mass, which saw it as a work which gained merit before God. Increasingly, however, Luther's writings on this subject changed their focus. Rather than defining his position over and against Rome, he now had to defend his other flank, as he came under attack from colleagues within the Reformation itself. Luther always believed that Christ was truly, physically present in the bread and wine of the eucharist. For him, it was impossible to think of Christ being present only 'spiritually'. In Christ, God took on human flesh and blood and if Christ was present at all, he had to be present in physical form. Yet this was as far as he was prepared to go. As he wrote in 1527: 'In the supper we eat and take to ourselves Christ's body truly and physically. But how this takes place or how he is in the bread, we do not know and are not meant to know.' Transubstantiation was for Luther a theory which tried to express the inexpressible. It was not so much wrong, as unnecessary. It was not in the Bible, but came from the ideas of Aristotle who, after all, was not even a Christian. Moreover, it had encouraged excessive fascination with the elements themselves, distracting attention from Christ. All the same, Luther held firmly and stubbornly to the idea of the 'real presence' of Christ in the eucharist. As we have seen, this had already been a bone of contention with Karlstadt in Wittenberg, but now it began to loom large as a dispute which threatened to split the evangelical movement right down the middle.

After his early tangles with Karlstadt on the issue, Luther heard rumours that some of the Swiss reformers took a similar view of the holy communion as merely a reminder of Christ's death on the cross. Oecolampadius in Basel, Martin Bucer in Strasbourg, and Huldrych Zwingli in Zürich all denied that Christ was physically present in the eucharist. Not for the first time, Luther jumped to the conclusion that they were all saying roughly the same thing, and that they had been infected directly by Karlstadt's teaching. In fact, as Luther was later to discover, they all took subtly different positions on the issue, and had had little contact with Karlstadt. Yet over this one question there was clear water between Luther and the Swiss: was Christ physically present in the elements or not?

As ever, Luther was more interested in defending true doctrine than looking for a compromise solution. For some years, brief and inconclusive theological skirmishes took place between the two sides. Eventually, both Luther and Zwingli were persuaded to publish heavyweight defences of their views, which appeared alongside each other at the Frankfurt Book Fair in spring 1527. Battle positions were being taken up, forces arrayed, argument and counter-arguments mustered and, for all the words which poured off the presses, the two sides seemed as far apart as ever.

> 'The Spirit cannot be with us except in material and physical things such as the word, water and Christ's body and in his saints on earth.'
>
> **Martin Luther, *That These Words of Christ, 'This is My Body,' etc., Still Stand Firm Against the Fanatics*, 1527**

In the 16th century, no matter could remain purely theological for long. Soon, political interests began to influence events. Reform-minded princes, increasingly anxious about the threat of Catholic armies, sought to arrange an alliance of evangelical cities and rulers to defend the Reformation cause. Early in 1529, an imperial Diet at Speyer introduced strong measures to restrict the spread of evangelical ideas, reinforcing the edicts of the Diet of Worms, which had never properly been implemented. Some evangelical princes and cities were provoked enough to issue an official 'protest' to the absent emperor, giving birth to the nickname 'Protestants'. One such prince was Philip of Hesse, a young, able, but headstrong, leader who, by 1528, was convinced of the importance of a united Protestant military front. The problem which stood in the way was that the theologians could not agree with one another. And the issue which divided them above all was that of the eucharist.

Philip decided that the only way forward was to bring together the disputants to thrash out their differences. In June 1529, he sent out invitations to the major figures in the debate between the Wittenbergers and the Swiss. They were to come to his castle in Marburg for a 'colloquy', or conversation, with a view to settling their differences. Luther was unimpressed. The year before, he had published what he thought was his last word on the subject, his *Confession Concerning Christ's Supper*. He was sure he had read scripture correctly, and saw no point in arguing further. At best, he might convince Zwingli and the others, but he saw little prospect of that. At worst, the debate would end in stalemate, an outcome which could only harm, not help, the evangelical cause. As he wrote to his own Elector John, who had succeeded Frederick the Wise after the latter's death in 1525: 'All conferences are wasted and all meetings are in vain if both parties come to them with no intention of yielding anything.' Luther had, by now, been to too many Diets, disputations and colloquies to expect much from them.

On the other hand, to refuse would mean driving the influential Philip into the hands of the Swiss. Zwingli and Oecolampadius had already accepted their invitations, so Luther and Melanchthon eventually and reluctantly agreed to make the 200-mile trip to Marburg. They set out on 17 September 1529, along with Justus Jonas, Caspar Cruciger, and George Rörer, Luther's secretary. Thirteen days later, they arrived in Marburg, where Zwingli, Oecolampadius, Bucer and Hedio on the Swiss side had already settled into their quarters in the castle. On their arrival, Oecolampadius and Bucer greeted the men from Wittenberg warmly. This was a good start, even if Luther jestingly did call Bucer a rascal for his crafty editorial methods in the debate so far. Zwingli, dressed in black, wearing a sword as usual, hung back from the welcome, perhaps anticipating the sharpness of the contest to come. Two days later, the deputation of Lutherans from southern Germany arrived, including Osiander, Brenz and Agricola. Never before had such a gathering of key figures in the Reformation taken place. It is ironic that it was not unity, but disagreement that brought them together.

For two full days, from six o'clock on the morning of Saturday 2 October until late on Sunday evening, the summit meeting continued. The theologians spoke in German, so that Philip and other assembled nobles could follow. For the most part, the debate proceeded without animosity although, just occasionally, the tension broke out into angry words. Once, Zwingli darkly threatened that his arguments would break Luther's neck. 'Don't boast too much,' retorted Luther sharply, 'Necks don't break that easily here – remember you are in Hesse, not in Switzerland.'

> 'Then for his own benefit, he wrote the text, "This is my body," on the table with a piece of chalk.'
>
> **Report of Osiander at the Marburg Colloquy, 1529**

Luther and Zwingli both took their stand on particular verses of scripture. Zwingli's central text was John 6:63: 'It is the Spirit that gives life, the flesh is of no avail.' For him, God is spirit, and works in a directly spiritual way upon the human soul. The human soul is nourished by spiritual, not physical, food, so Christ's physical presence in the bread and wine is not only distasteful, but unnecessary. Zwingli was anxious that Luther's clinging on to the old medieval idea of the 'real presence' still meant that ordinary believers would focus too much attention on the physical elements and not on the spiritual reality of Christ. For Zwingli, Christ's human body was, in principle, distinct from his divine, spiritual nature. Christ's human body, now it had ascended, was now at the right hand of God, and so could not be here on earth in bread and wine.

Luther, however, rested on Christ's words at the last supper: 'This is my body.' Luther would often chalk up texts or sayings he wanted to remember on walls and even furniture, so it was no surprise to his friends when, early in the debate, he wrote the Latin words *Hoc est corpus meum* on the table in the large living room of the castle where the colloquy took place, and repeatedly pointed back to them. For him, these words were plain. Jesus indicated that the bread literally contained his body. To avoid this obvious meaning of the text, as Zwingli was trying to do, was to twist the meaning of scripture to suit his own ends. Zwingli had interpreted John 6:63 to mean that God only works through spiritual not physical realities. This, argued Luther, was, in effect, to deny the incarnation. If God does not work through physical matter, how and why, then, had he chosen deliberately to reveal himself and to work out the salvation of the world through the incarnate Christ, with his embarrassingly physical body and human flesh? In any case, wasn't Zwingli's preference for the spiritual over the physical more a pagan Greek idea than a Christian, scriptural one? Did it not limit God's power to insist that after the ascension Christ's body could not be in the bread and wine because it was in heaven with God? Surely, if God so wished, Christ's body could be anywhere and everywhere?

Huldrych Zwingli

Born in 1484, Huldrych Zwingli was one of the major leaders in the early years of the Reformation in Switzerland. He studied in Basel, Bern and the University of Vienna, where he came into contact with humanist ideas, which had a profound and lasting effect on his thinking. He arrived at reforming views similar to Luther's before encountering Luther's works, whilst he was a pastor in Glarus and Einsiedeln. He arrived in Zürich in 1519. There, during the early 1520s, his reforming agenda gradually gained the approval of the city council. He introduced new forms of church life, involving a bare, simple form of service, with no hymns, music or images, and the sermon as the centrepiece. Zwingli engaged in running arguments with the radical wing of the Reformation which took root early in Zürich. In line with his political theology, which saw church and state as two sides of the same coin, he was killed in 1531 near Kappel, defending Zürich in a skirmish against nearby Catholic states.

Far from opposing invisible spirit to physical flesh, Luther argued that John 6:63 did not mean what Zwingli said it did. It simply stated that 'our sinful and carnal being' was powerless to achieve salvation. Zwingli replied that when Jesus said 'this *is* my body', he was merely speaking metaphorically, and there could only be a spiritual eating of Christ's body in the eucharist.

'Tell Mr Pomer that the best arguments have been, in Zwingli's case, that a body cannot exist without a location, therefore Christ's body is not in the bread, and in Oecolampadius's case, that this sacrament is a sign of Christ's body. I assume that God has blinded them so that they had nothing else to offer.'

Martin Luther to his wife, Katie, from Marburg, October 1529

The arguments flowed back and forth over texts from the Bible and quotations from early church Fathers. As the two sides jostled and manoeuvred, impressions were formed. On Luther's side, Justus Jonas found Zwingli 'boorish and presumptuous', Oecolampadius the epitome of charm and kindness, Hedio 'refined and broadminded', Bucer as crafty as a fox. Luther was quick-witted and stubborn, Melanchthon gentle and precise.

Towards Sunday evening it became clear that neither side was prepared to give ground on the crucial question. A measure of urgency crept in when the news entered the castle that an outbreak of a fatal disease known as 'English Sweat' had occurred in the town. The participants had to depart hastily, so a statement was quickly drawn up. On 14 out of 15 articles there was agreement. On the 15th article, 'Concerning the Sacrament of the Body and Blood of Christ', six separate points were made. On the first five, both sides agreed. On the sixth, final and central point, they were as far apart as ever: 'We have not yet reached an agreement as to whether the true body and blood of Christ are bodily present in the bread and wine, nevertheless, each side should show Christian love to the other side insofar as conscience will permit, and both sides should diligently pray to Almighty God that through his Spirit he might confirm in us the right understanding.'

The friendly tone could not disguise the gulf which lay between them. Luther had claimed that the Swiss had a 'different spirit', one where the words of Christ were 'censured, resisted, regarded as false and attacked'. The Swiss had accused the Germans of being 'eaters of human flesh, worshippers of a God of bread, a baked God'. They departed determined to be friends, yet their failure to reach agreement set both movements on separate trajectories which continue to this day. Within a decade, Germany was split geographically between the Lutheran north and east, and the Reformed south and west. The Marburg Colloquy ended on a note of muted sadness. The theological argument was not the sole cause of the divide, but it helped create a persistent fault-line in the Protestant world. It opened a wound which refused to heal, weakened the movement and prevented it from presenting a united spiritual, theological or military front in the fierce struggles that were to come.

> 'Our spirit is different from yours; it is clear that we do not possess the same spirit, for it cannot be the same spirit when in one place the words of Christ are simply believed and in another place the same faith is censured, resisted, regarded as false and attacked with all kinds of malicious and blasphemous words.'
>
> **Martin Luther, at the Marburg Colloquy, 1529**

CHAPTER 8

The Patriarch

From the beginning, Luther had opposed the papacy as much for what it had failed to do as for what it had done. It had neglected the flock of Christ, and had left it starving for the true spiritual food, which was the gospel of faith. It was never enough to win the academic arguments; there was also the task of putting the Reformation into practice in the churches that had adopted Luther's reforming programme up and down Germany, and imprinting it on the hearts of individuals. The danger had always been, as had happened in Wittenberg during Luther's stay in the Wartburg, that his simplified form of Christianity would be interpreted either as licence to rip up everything connected to the old ways, or to abandon all religious practice and replace it with nothing but an invisible inner religion.

'Luther's concern for the church... remained intact, and the papacy became its first major casualty.'

Scott Hendrix, *Luther and the Papacy*, 1981

Since the early 1520s, Luther had written a whole series of liturgies, hymns and services for his new style of church, from a Latin *Order of Mass and Communion for the Church In Wittenberg*, composed after the disturbances there had died down in 1523, to a *German Mass and Order of Service*, written in 1526 for ordinary people who did not understand Latin, the language of church services up to this point. Alongside these, a German baptismal service was written and, soon, orders of marriage, confession and ordination followed, along with a *Small Catechism* in 1529.

Luther had been badgering the Elector John to do something about the state of the churches and the clergy in Saxony. Luther's idea was to run an official visitation of the churches, to find out

what was actually happening in the parishes, both on financial and religious fronts. The visitation began in 1527, and it quickly became apparent that the visitors needed clear instructions. Melanchthon drafted some which, incidentally, brought about quite a sharp disagreement with Agricola on the relationship between faith and repentance, which Luther had to help to sort out. The final version, published in 1528, was heavily worked over by Luther, and provides a fascinating and typical example of Luther's approach to church reform, in its advice to pastors.

Pastors are primarily to be preachers, not Mass-providers, like the priests of the old church. The message of the forgiveness of sins, 'not on account of merits, but on account of Christ', is to be repeated again and again in their sermons, until everyone gets the point. Prayer will normally use set forms, such as the Lord's Prayer, but is not to be done without careful thought and attention to the words being said. Especially in large towns, daily services, often sung with scriptural canticles and German hymns, are to be held in the churches every morning and evening. Clergy are to urge parents to send their children to Christian schools. Reflecting humanist aspirations, Luther recommends a simple syllabus, which includes learning Latin and reading Aesop's fables, Terence's plays and Ovid's poetry. Music, grammar and rhetoric are to be taught to the best students, and one day a week is to be kept aside for Christian instruction – learning to recite the Ten Commandments, the Lord's Prayer and the Creed. The teacher is to drum into his pupils the three essential components for living a good life: 'The fear of God, faith, good works.'

> 'Thank God a child of seven knows what the church is – the holy believers and the lambs who hear their shepherd's voice.'
>
> **Martin Luther,** *Schmalkaldic Articles*, **1537**

Throughout, there is the cultivation of a freely chosen set of outward forms, including liturgies, festivals and saints days (though saints are not to be prayed to: 'A competent preacher ought to be able to show how to celebrate the festivals without superstition.'). However, the lesson is constantly emphasized – these are to be used, 'not in order to earn grace or to make satisfaction for sins, but because they serve a useful purpose'. In some respects, the orders of service looked similar to those in the old church, translated into German. In Wittenberg's city church, the host was still elevated during the communion until 1542, the choir still sang much of the service, and the clergy were still robed. Yet the spirit and motivation was meant to be entirely different

Unlike the reform programmes of some of the more radical groups of the time, Luther's Reformation never despised the role of outward forms, regular acts of public prayer and devotion which were to structure and punctuate the day in offerings of confession and praise to God. This was how faith was nurtured, learned and kept alive. This was not just an inner invisible devotion, but was to be regularly expressed in visible and audible forms.

> 'The people are to be taught that the only reason for keeping these festivals is to learn the word of God.'
>
> **Martin Luther,** *Instructions for Visitors of Parish Pastors,* 1528

In later life, Luther was often disappointed at the practical results of the reforms. Stories reached him of those who had rejected the old faith, but had not replaced it with anything better. Morals did not seem to improve a great deal, and even in Wittenberg he became depressed at how shallow faith was. People still drank too much, the local brothel still thrived, and women's fashions took on a more seductive style. In 1545, whilst he was away ordaining a bishop in Merseburg, a story reached him of an adulterous affair which had scandalized Wittenberg. In a fit of despair, he wrote to say that he was not coming back. He was giving up on them. Katie should move to the farm he had bought her in Zölsdorf to prepare for her widowhood and to carry on without him. Not unusually, Luther was exaggerating. His theology and reform had spread across Europe, and had even become the official religion of many regions. Some did live exemplary lives guided by his teaching. Yet, by this stage, as papal and imperial power was growing and the progress of reform often looked slow, at times everything could seem bleak.

Since the controversy with the papacy, Luther was so afraid of reintroducing justification by works through the back door that he emphasized that everything in true Christian life must be undertaken freely without compulsion. This, however, could give the impression, not just that everything was free, but that everything was optional. He was always reluctant to impose discipline, requirements and firm structures, in case people mistook these for ways of achieving salvation. Perhaps this explains some of the lack of fervency in the 'Lutheran' churches at the time. The new churches developing in the Reformed tradition in Switzerland, under the guidance of new figures such as John Calvin and Martin Bucer, had fewer qualms about order and discipline. These churches proved more durable under conditions of persecution in the years to come, and spread more easily from the grassroots.

> 'From this period on, Luther was to shrink his expectations and if anything, see life as darker, God as more mysterious, and inscrutable, and Satan as more active.'
>
> Richard Marius, *Martin Luther: The Christian Between God and Death*, 1999

Politics again

As the 1530s began, the fears which had lurked around the Marburg Colloquy proved well founded. After several years of political limbo, things were beginning to move again. The divide between the evangelicals and the papal church had spread far beyond Germany into Switzerland and the Netherlands, and even further north into Scandinavia. The 1529 Diet of Speyer, with its demand that the Edict of Worms be finally implemented, had severely concentrated the minds of the evangelicals. Now it was rumoured that the emperor was keen to take up the issues again. He was said to be planning another imperial Diet, the first time he would be personally present since Worms. It would meet in the wealthy city of Augsburg, which held memories for Luther of his earlier encounter with Cajetan. This time, however, Luther was not allowed to be there. As a heretic, under papal condemnation and the imperial ban, he could not appear before the emperor again.

Despite what had happened at Speyer, Charles's tone was positive as the Diet approached. Again, foreign policy dictated internal policy – just as 10 years before, the Turkish threat meant that Charles could not afford a divided Europe, and this made him less keen on aggressive action against the 'Protestants'. He made it known that he was keen to give a hearing to all sides in the debate on reform. The Elector John was even more an avid supporter of Luther, and certainly more inclined to action than his elder brother. When he was summoned to the Diet, he asked the Wittenberg theologians to begin compiling a statement of their theological position. The plan was for Melanchthon and Jonas to go to Augsburg itself; Luther would stay at nearby Coburg, within reach if they needed him.

Luther settled into his quarters in the large, roomy Coburg Castle, perched on a hill above the city, just like Marburg, on 24 April 1530. He was agitated and anxious, unable to sleep well on the first night. Large flocks of jackdaws circled around the airy building. Their noisy gathering reminded Luther of the knights, noblemen and churchmen arriving at Augsburg at the time. As soon as he arrived at Coburg, Luther set to writing his own *Exhortation to all Clergy Assembled at Augsburg*, finishing it on 5 May 1530 and sending it off to be published at Wittenberg. In it, he retold the story of the past 15 or so years, claiming that not only had he rid the bishops of the monks, but that he had also saved the papacy and the estates from the uprising of the peasants. Towards the end he comes to the point. His offer is to let them be, if they will let him be. Luther will happily let the bishops exercise episcopal jurisdiction, if only they will cease persecuting the evangelicals and let them get on with preaching their gospel freely. It will cost them nothing, because Luther's churches intend to be self-supporting. The bishops can administer, and the evangelicals will preach, teach and

reform churches. Characteristically, the piece is full of Luther's habitual abuse, name-calling and criticism. The papal church has allowed trivia such as indulgences, the veneration of saints, processions and cowls to crowd out the really important things such as the gospel, grace, faith and liberty. By silencing Luther, it has silenced the gospel. Despite his conciliatory offer, it was not a treatise likely to bring peace!

It felt as if the fate of the whole evangelical reform movement was in the balance, and Luther could do nothing. He had every confidence in Melanchthon's theological prowess, and had no doubt that he could make a precise and accurate statement of their position, as he had already done in his already well-known *Loci Communes*. He was also aware of Philipp's more timid nature, and how easily he had been swayed in the past by Karlstadt and the prophets from Zwickau. The Elector John was a good ally, but no theologian, and Luther feared that in his absence, they would give too much ground. Frustrated that he could not be there, Luther spent much of the time worrying about how things were going. He was plagued by his usual enemies in times of stress: bad constipation, severe headaches, doubt and spiritual *Anfechtungen*. He bombarded Melanchthon, Spalatin and the others in Augsburg with letters. Some were tetchy and sulky, complaining about the lack of news. Others were grand and rich, encouraging Duke John to live up to his name of 'the Steadfast' by preserving the paradise which God had given him to govern in Saxony, where the gospel was freely taught and children grew up to know a good and gracious God.

During his stay in Coburg Castle, an old friend from Magdeburg days arrived with news of Luther's father's death. When he heard it, Luther took hold of his copy of the Psalms, and locked himself into his room, not emerging for a whole day. Thinking back on all he owed to his father, and no doubt recalling the episode of his entry into the monastery, where his father's doubts had been truer than his own conviction, his tears flowed freely. Luther confessed to being 'shaken in the innermost parts of my being, so that seldom if ever have I despised death as much as I do now'.

Meanwhile, at Augsburg, the Wittenbergers continued to work on their statement. Melanchthon skilfully worked the articles they had prepared beforehand into a 28-point statement, which became known as the *Augsburg Confession*. It remains a definitive statement of Lutheran faith to this day. Unlike Luther, Melanchthon still hoped and believed that some kind of agreement with the papal church was possible. The *Confession*, therefore, was written in a much more conciliatory tone than if Luther had been its author. Melanchthon frequently pointed out where Lutheran doctrine was the same as that of his opponents, and he was careful to distance himself from the more radical wing of the Reformation movement which had continued alongside and beyond the peasants' revolt. When Luther finally received a copy, he declared himself 'tremendously pleased with it' although, perhaps predictably, he remained unconvinced by his colleague's moderate and appeasing approach.

At the Diet, despite the machinations of the papalists to prevent it, Melanchthon's *Confession*, signed by the Elector John, Philip of Hesse and seven other Protestant princes, was read out on Saturday 25 June 1530 by Christian Beier, the Elector's Vice-Chancellor. The day was warm, and some bystanders swore later on that the emperor, who could not understand German, dozed off during the two-hour long reading. When Luther heard, he was delighted that he had lived to see the day when his gospel had been publicly presented before the highest secular court in Europe. Other evangelicals could not agree with the Wittenbergers' statement,

'That at Augsburg kings sovereigns and people are raging and howling against the Anointed of the Lord I consider to be a good sign, and much better than if they were flattering.'

Martin Luther to Georg Spalatin, from Coburg, 30 June 1530

'Pray... for the emperor, that excellent young man... And then also for our sovereign, who is not less good yet carries a heavier cross, and for Philipp, who miserably tortures himself with worries.'

Martin Luther to Conrad Cordatus, from Coburg, 6 July 1530

including Zwingli's party from Switzerland, and a combined group from Strasbourg, Constance, Memmingen and Lindau, who produced their own version, the *Confessio Tetrapolitana*. Some of the papal bishops seemed quietly impressed, but they were in the minority. The key players on the papal side, the Italian Cardinal Campeggio and Luther's old adversary Johann Eck, were keen to ensure that the emperor would not move. They engaged not so much in theological argument – again, Luther's ideas were not destined to be debated – but in simple denunciation. During the next few weeks, discussions continued, and the letters kept arriving from Coburg, urging Melanchthon, Duke John and the others to stand firm.

Eventually, the imperial verdict was pronounced on 22 September. It was the result that Charles had always intended giving. He called for a council of the church but, meanwhile, demanded that the Protestants conform to 'the holy faith and the Christian religion', by which he meant the papal church. They had six months to comply. Melanchthon's hopes were dashed, Luther's expectations fulfilled. Duke John and his party left abruptly, picked up Luther from Coburg on the way home, and were soon back home in Saxony.

> 'The Augsburg Confession, because of its historical importance and doctrinal weight, rapidly became the definitive confession for Lutherans.'
>
> **Mark Noll, *Confessions and Catechisms of the Reformation*, 1991**

The Diet of Augsburg marked the end of any realistic hopes for reconciliation between the 'Catholics' and the newly designated 'Protestants'. From now on, the united Christendom of Europe was to be publicly fractured, and the different churches were to go their own way. Melanchthon never quite gave up hope and later, in 1540, he engaged in a dialogue with a conciliatory Italian cardinal, Contarini, at Regensburg. Remarkably they managed to agree on a form of words on justification, but both had conceded too much for their respective masters, and the agreement never stuck. A year after Augsburg, the Elector John signed up to a Protestant defensive coalition, the Schmalkaldic

League, formed to defend their territories against possible papal attack. Despite Luther's misgivings about violence, he reluctantly gave his blessing to the idea. Against such a large body, the emperor could do no more than negotiate, and the break-up of Europe into religious and political power blocks began. Europe's church was now split, and it remains so today. The imperial attack was not to come until after Luther's death. Charles left Germany in 1532, and did not return for another 10 years, during which Luther's reform programme began to spread wider and deeper.

Life in Wittenberg

All the struggles had taken their toll. As he approached 50, Luther's health began to suffer from the volume of work and the battles being fought on every side. 1527 was a particularly bad year for Luther. In July that year, he was struck by a severe episode of spiritual *Anfechtung* and physical illness, which often coincided. Not only were the papacy, the peasants and the emperor against him, there was now the opposition from the radical 'enthusiasts' and the Swiss over the sacraments. As his sense of terror and doubt grew and Bugenhagen, the parish minister, was called to absolve him, Jonas listened to Luther's fears as they walked around Jonas's garden, before returning to Luther's own house, the old friary. When they arrived there, Luther felt worse, went to bed and prepared to die. A physician was called, who treated him with hot compresses. Gradually, the terror passed, though it would return periodically for the coming years.

Later that same year, the plague hit Wittenberg. Most students and many of the university faculty left the town. Luther, as pastor, stayed behind, and the home turned into a hospital for the sick and dying. George Rörer's wife, Hanna, died after giving birth to a stillborn child, and Luther's despair and depression continued. By December 1527, the plague had run its course, yet Luther's own trials still haunted him. In a letter to Jonas, now staying in Nordhausen, he asked, 'Do not cease praying for and struggling along with me, my Jonas, for sometimes my spiritual trials are weaker, but in time they return with even greater violence, so that Christ may not abandon me... and that my faith may not cease until the end.' In the early 1530s, Luther continued to experience fainting fits, kidney stones and pounding headaches and, in 1537, he nearly died from bladder problems, yet these lacked the severe spiritual depression experienced in 1527.

The rediscovery of the gospel had not banished the depressions Luther had experienced in the monastery in Erfurt, but they had given him a means of coping with them. His most fearful temptation was to doubt that God was really good. In fact, his whole life might be characterized as a struggle with the possibility that God might actually turn out to be the devil. Sitting at table with a group of younger students in 1533, Luther warned them: 'Beware of melancholy... Our God has commanded us to be cheerful... My temptation is this, that I think I don't have a gracious God.' What if God really did wish him damned? What if God was malicious and tyrannical, imposing all kinds of impossible expectations upon sinners, and then damning them for being unable to meet the requirements? Over and against this, he would again and again turn to God's word, which assured him of God's goodness, despite all that suggested the contrary. The temptations would normally come thick and fast at night, when he tossed and turned beside Katie, plagued by devilish thoughts. Sometimes a glass or two of beer before retiring to bed would help him to sleep better; sometimes he would argue with the devil, flinging God's words at him to make him go away. Turning over in bed and farting at the devil was sometimes an effective means of making him depart! Luther's theology was never an academic exercise – it was

> 'My lord Katie... drives the wagon, takes care of the fields, buys and puts cattle out to pasture, brews etc. In between she has started to read the Bible, and I have promised her 50 gulden if she finishes before Easter.'
>
> **Martin Luther, in a letter to Justus Jonas, 1535**

forged in the furnace of spiritual and physical pain. A test of any theology is whether in times of great distress it provides comfort and strength, or whether it proves irrelevant and useless. If this is a true test, Luther's theology passed with flying colours.

Through all of this, Luther continued his programme of preaching up to four times a week, lecturing in the university, dealing with the pastoral concerns of Wittenberg's citizens, writing books and keeping in touch with events on a Europe-wide canvas. The energetic Katie looked after the house more than ably. She bought a small plot of land outside the Elster gate and brewed her own beer. In 1532, the Elector John formally gave to the couple the deeds to the former Augustinian friary – it was now officially Luther's home.

The house was busy and full. Five children arrived: three boys – John, Martin and Paul – and two daughters. Both daughters, however, died young: Elizabeth in 1528, aged only eight months, and Magdalena, whose death at the age of 13 caused Luther and Katie such 'crying and grieving' that 'even the death of Christ is not able to take all this away as it should'.

The house was seldom quiet. To make ends meet, Katie had to take in students as lodgers. The large family room at the heart of the house, with its wooden panelling and large porcelain oven, was the scene of countless conversations and discussions. Some would jot down the more memorable of the great man's sayings, sometimes to his annoyance, and subsequently publish them – these were to become the famous and still very entertaining and evocative 'Table Talk'. Luther's old friends Melanchthon, Bugenhagen, Jonas, Amsdorf, Rörer, Cranach and the others were all regular visitors. Official guests came from further afield – princes, delegates from other Reformed cities, emissaries from as far away as England asking for Luther's advice and help in the matter of the new king Henry VIII's plans to divorce his first wife, and even the odd cardinal.

Luther and Katie's marriage was strong, genial and satisfying. Letters between them are full of jokes, endearments and affection – here were two good friends as well as companions. They would argue vigorously and fish together on the nearby River Elbe. Luther would tease Katie for talking too much; she would jokingly threaten to go back to the convent. She was financially much more astute than him, and would occasionally rebuke him for his reckless generosity and refusal to accept payment for his books or teaching. After all, she was the one who had to make ends meet and keep the visitors fed. Luther clearly enjoyed home life, and found in it all kinds of reminders of God. Katie's blazing oven reminded him of God as a blazing furnace of love; his dog Tölpel fixed its eyes intently on a piece of meat which his master was holding, not allowing himself to be distracted by anything – 'If only I could pray the way this dog watches the meat!' said Luther.

Never one to sit idle, while fretting in Coburg about the proceedings at Augsburg, Luther had got down to the translation of the Old Testament again. Now back in Wittenberg he had the help of Melanchthon the Greek expert, Matthew Aurogallus, the Professor of Hebrew, and his old friend the Professor of Theology, Caspar Cruciger. This group translation was, for Luther, a labour of love. Sometimes they could only manage three lines of Hebrew a day. To get the details right on the Old Testament sacrificial system, Luther would wander down to the local Wittenberg butchers to ask the correct names for the different parts of animal intestines. He would peer into the nearby forests to make sure that he had identified the birds of the Bible correctly.

When the complete German Bible appeared in 1534, Luther was proud of the result. If all his books were to be burned, the one he would choose to survive was the German Bible. Given the choice, he would always abandon strict word-for-word translation of the Hebrew in order to achieve a good, earthy German phrase. Not only was he proud that he had made Moses, Jeremiah and Paul speak like Saxons, he also boasted that this was even better and more theologically reliable than the Latin

Vulgate, the great Bible of St Jerome, which had served the whole church for centuries.

Healing the rifts

Attempts were still being made to heal the division caused by the Reformation in Europe. With the emperor, as ever, needing support to fight the menacing Turks, a truce was engineered between Protestants and Papalists, the 1532 'Peace of Nuremberg', of which Luther approved. Even though Zwingli was now dead, killed while defending Zürich in a battle against local Catholic forces, the eucharistic debate which had reached stalemate at Marburg was still alive. Although Luther had few hopes that the issue could be resolved, and resorted to flinging the occasional volley at his opponents in Switzerland, Martin Bucer, a tireless peacemaker in the evangelical ranks, was still trying to find a solution. The efforts issued in an agreed statement, the *Wittenberg Concord*, signed in 1536 after intensive discussions and diplomatic visits by the Wittenbergers, and by Bucer and Capito, Strasbourg reformers. The statement preserved Luther's insistence on a real presence of Christ in the elements, but clarified that this did not mean a cannibalistic eating of flesh. This was still not enough for the Swiss, however, and despite friendlier relations in the early 1540s, the two sides never could reach agreement.

> 'This German Bible is clearer and more accurate at many points than the Latin... if the printers do not as usual spoil it with their carelessness, the German language certainly has here a better Bible than the Latin language – and the readers will bear me out on this.'
>
> **Martin Luther, preface to the German Bible, 1534**

Even further away was the growing problem of the radical wing of the Reformation movement. Luther never bought into the idea that just because the papacy was corrupt, everything had to be overturned. In a 1528 piece, *Concerning Rebaptism*, he had written: 'We on our part confess that there is much that is Christian and good under the papacy; indeed everything that is Christian and good is to be found there and has come to

us from this source.' (He meant, of course, such things as the Bible, the sacraments, the Ten Commandments and the Lord's Prayer). His main argument was with their refusal to listen, and the attempt to silence and persecute the gospel. Nor could he abide the underhand lawlessness he perceived in the Anabaptist groups. He felt that their leaders were self-appointed, subversive and lawless, not recognizing the true and legal authorities in both church and state, going about their business stealthily and secretly. It has to be said that they had little choice, because they were as likely to be persecuted by Protestant princes as much as by Catholic ones. Luther's judgment was not altogether informed, but rather based on surmises and preconceptions, because he had little first-hand knowledge of these groups. Their willingness to be a minority in what they saw as a wider un-Christian society arguably anticipated the church in the West in coming centuries more accurately than the state churches bequeathed by Luther and the mainstream reformers.

By the 1540s, Luther's writings were punctuated with weary resignation. Philip of Hesse had extracted reluctant support from Luther, Melanchthon and Bucer for a bigamous marriage to his mistress. The subsequent storm did all their reputations no good. Luther's continuing illnesses, and a desire for the end, perhaps explain two of his most extraordinary outbursts during these years. One concerned Henry of Wolfenbüttel, an implacable Catholic opponent of the Reformation, whose sexual morals were even worse than Philip of Hesse's, and who had suspicious links with outbreaks of arson in some Protestant towns. When he insulted the Elector John Frederick of Saxony, who had now succeeded his father John the Steadfast who had died in 1532, Henry drew the fire of the master of insults, Martin Luther. Luther could write personal venom when he wanted to. In a broadside on Henry entitled *Against Hanswurst* (1541), Luther did not hold back. The language is colourful, at times funny, shocking and rude. The 16th century frequently saw crude and acerbic language –

Thomas Müntzer and William Shakespeare provide other notable examples – and Luther could produce it as eloquently as any.

Even worse was a cantankerous and ill-tempered attack on the Jews in 1543. In earlier days, Luther had seemed more favourable than most to the Jews, in what was a largely anti-Semitic society. He had favoured the use of Jewish scholars in establishing Hebrew grammar, a controversial position at the time, and his *That Jesus was Born a Jew* of 1523 had reaffirmed Jesus' Jewishness when others were embarrassed by it. At that point, he was clearly hoping for a wholesale conversion of Jews, now that the gospel had been rediscovered.

Anabaptists

After the peasants' revolt, many on the more radical wing of the reforming movement, no longer looking to Luther for support, had begun to form small, independent groupings in cities throughout the continent. Similar movements had begun further south, especially in the area around Zürich, where they were a thorn in the flesh of Zwingli, and to the north-west, into the Netherlands. Despite an abortive and violent attempt by one group to seize power in Münster in north-west Germany in 1534, most of these were quiet gatherings of peaceful people, earnestly seeking a more radical and spiritualized way of expressing Christian life. They often shared their possessions in community, many of them were pacifist, and all of them practised adult, not infant, baptism (hence the name often given to them – Ana- [re-] Baptists).

Now he was getting older. It is a feature of his later years that he became less hopeful of change, less willing to discuss and more prone to angry polemic. Even the news of a forthcoming council of the church – the famous Council of Trent, which began in 1545 – was met with derision and disdain. He could entertain no hope at all that any council would make the changes he had demanded. He was now too world-weary for that. When he read a Jewish tract designed to convert Christians, his capacity for hatred reared its head. *On the Jews and their Lies* is a long, wordy

piece, alternating biblical interpretation with the repetition of medieval superstitions and fear about Jewish malice. It ends with a notorious section in which Luther advocates the burning of Jewish synagogues, homes and books, their reduction to a form of serfdom, and their final expulsion from the land. There are few mitigating factors in all this. It can be said that he was only repeating what many before him had suggested, that this was an old and irritable man writing in frustration at his opponents, and that at least he provided no grounds for the wholesale extermination of the Jews as was advocated by another German regime 400 years later. However, his words were used fatefully by the Nazis and are a strong corrective to those who want to make Luther a hero too uncritically.

In 1546, he found himself, not unusually, involved in a dispute over inheritance rights between the counts of Mansfeld, the city where his parents had lived. Visits there were tiring, but eventually successful. On the final visit to Eisleben in February, after all parties had happily made peace, Luther stayed on to sort out the final details. While preaching in the parish church of St Andrew, he stumbled over his words and could not continue. He was taken down from the pulpit, and led just a few yards across the street to his lodgings. In an upstairs room early in the morning of 18 February, accompanied by a small group, including Justus Jonas and his own sons, he died of a stroke, possibly a heart attack, in a house just a few hundred yards from the one where he was born. His last written words were: 'We are beggars – that is the truth of it.'

'Hanswurst, how you lie! Oh Harry Wolfenbüttel, what a shameless liar you are! You spout a lot, but you say nothing. You slander, but you prove nothing. This kind of art is performed by the arch-prostitute in the street when she calls an honest virgin a drab, a whore, a harlot, and a strumpet... It would cause such a prostitute no great effort to give utterance to a book like the one our Hanswurst of Wolfenbüttel has written.'

Martin Luther, *Against Hanswurst*, 1541

CHAPTER 9

The Legacy

As we come to the end of his story, Martin Luther's life and the vast impact his actions and beliefs have had upon the development of the Western world call for some assessment. How do we interpret this complex character and his legacy in the present?

One recent biographer calls Luther 'a catastrophe in the history of Western civilization'. If one looks only at the legacy of religious wars and division which were part of the aftermath of the Reformation, then such a verdict is hard to avoid. When we place against that, however, Luther's role in recalling the church to a simpler, more egalitarian and communal vision, and in puncturing the conceited abuse of power and hierarchical oppressiveness of an institution which most now agree had become corrupt, not to mention the inspiration which his theology has been to countless people over past centuries, the judgment does not seem so fair.

> 'By comparison with traditional practice, the Reformation radically simplified religious life – a change still visible today.'
>
> **Stephen Ozment,** *Protestants*, 1993

Luther was a man of immense personal courage, fierce intelligence and Teutonic stubbornness. A mind steeped in the theology of his time, an ability to see through to the nub of an issue very quickly, and a facility with language that enabled him to express his ideas with clarity and popular vigour was a powerful mixture. As a man, he inspired deep loyalty and even love. He had a capacity to enjoy life hugely. He could be both tender and sharp, and his absence left an irreplaceable gap. As Melanchthon put it at his funeral, now they were 'entirely poor, wretched, forsaken, orphans who had lost a dear noble man as our father'. At the same time, Luther was a man with

deep flaws, who made enemies as quickly as he made friends, and whose brilliant language could be used to hurt as deeply as it could heal.

The trauma of his stand against the papacy perhaps explains a great deal of the later story. It is hard for us to imagine what it must have meant to stand alone against powerful and unbending institutions, knowing that if he was wrong, an eternity of agonizing pain reserved for heretics awaited him. In his struggle to find a good God, he had found a theology which could help him to stand against the great enemies of sin, death and hell – and he was not willing to be shifted from that one iota, even if it meant the full fury of emperor and pope. After this heroic stand, however, it seems that he gave up, not just on the papacy, but also on discussion. After Leipzig, Augsburg and Worms, he no longer thought that compromise could achieve anything. He found himself locked into an absolutism which meant that he could not engage with any of his opponents, be they the peasants, Erasmus, Zwingli or anyone else. It is as if he learned that stubborn and vociferous resistance was the only way to achieve anything, and he could not appreciate any other tactic. He would often say how he had no personal malice against his opponents, but rather against the spirit which he saw in them. In other words, he thought that he could see the same evil spirit which wanted to attack the word of God and faith lurking behind all his adversaries. If you think your opponents are inspired by the devil, it does make discussion and compromise rather difficult!

'Their writings accomplish nothing because they refrain from chiding, biting and giving offence.'

Martin Luther, on the writings of Erasmus and Capito, in a letter to Georg Spalatin, September 1521

Heroic stands are necessary when under attack, but they are not what is needed to build something new, durable and inclusive. As a result of this, Luther's influence on the later Reformation was less than it might have been. The mantle passed to Calvin in Geneva, and to Zwingi and then Bullinger in Zürich, to try to establish a workable Christian society in the new world of the post-medieval era. It was Philipp Melanchthon, not Martin Luther, who was given the title *Praeceptor Germaniae*, the Teacher of Germany.

Whatever historical judgment we come to, Luther's theology has continued to stimulate, comfort and provoke for nearly 500 years. As this book closes, we look at some areas of contemporary life where Luther's insights still have vital things to say to us today.

The problem of suffering

After the Second World War, as Europe woke up to the nightmare of what had happened in modern, civilized Germany, many could not believe what had happened. The bewilderment was real, both for the winners and the losers. After the discovery of Auschwitz, Buchenwald and Belsen, the inevitable question was: 'Where was God when all this was happening?' Idealistic 19th-century optimism was no longer an option. Humankind was not improving all the time; God was not the benevolent father looking down paternally from on high, knowing nothing of pain and suffering. A new approach to theology was needed.

The 'Luther renaissance' of the 19th century

The year 1883 was the 400th anniversary of Luther's birth, and it coincided with a period of strong Prussian nationalism. Statues of the Reformer appeared in the towns with which he was associated, and it was decided to produce a new edition of the works of this most famous German. The resulting *Weimar Edition* remains the largest and most important edition of Luther's works today. This renewed interest in Luther research led to the discovery of a number of important documents, including his early lectures on the Psalms and the book of Romans, which enriched understanding of the young Luther. One of the key ideas these texts highlighted was Luther's 'theology of the cross', which was discussed in chapter 3. Scholars such as

Karl Holl (1866–1926) and Emanuel Hirsch (1888–1972) began a new era in Luther research, trying to locate him in his broader historical context, while at the same time relating his thought to modern questions.

143

THE LEGACY

In post-war Germany, many theologians turned to Luther's theology of the cross to find the resources to make sense of their shattering experiences of the previous few years. Jürgen Moltmann, one of the most prominent Protestant theologians of the late-20th century was a German prisoner of war, who emerged into post-war life with many questions about God and his relation to the world. As he sat in lectures on Luther and the Reformation in Göttingen in 1948–49, Moltmann began to make some sense of the wartime experience. The result was a number of important works, perhaps most influentially, *The Crucified God*, which first appeared in 1973. It used Luther's ideas of the God hidden, yet revealed in the cross of Christ, to develop a theology which could understand God's relationship to the injustice and pain of the world. Was God absent in Auschwitz? Luther's language about a God hidden in suffering, the apparent absence of God in the cross of Christ, yet his hidden presence in the suffering of Jesus, working through it the salvation of the world, generated ideas which began to make some sense of the experience.

In Japan, another country on the losing side of the war, Christian theologians also turned to Luther for help. Kazoh Kitamori, a Japanese theologian, wrote an important book called *Theology of the Pain of God*, in which he drew on Luther's thought to develop the notion of a God who embraces and forgives sinful people, despite the pain that causes him. In a world where the goodness of God is cast under a shadow by the increasing awareness of the pain and injustice of that world, this theology of the cross offered a profound sense that God works in and through, not despite, suffering. Luther's struggle to find a good God still had resonance in the present. Both of these theologians learned from Luther that to understand the

Christian God, you need to begin, as Staupitz once said to him, 'with the wounds of Christ'.

Justification by faith

Modern, or even postmodern culture is no longer dominated by questions of religious conscience. We do not tend to agonize, as Luther did, over where we can find a gracious God, or how we might prepare for God's grace. Yet even though we do not face the demand to obey a whole series of religious rules, many people do experience a constant demand to live up to standards of beauty set by the glamour industry, to levels of achievement set by business targets, or to standards of talent set by sporting success. Low self-esteem, or negative self-worth, is a persistent and difficult problem, occupying a great deal of time and energy on psychiatrists' couches.

Naturally, Luther was writing before the development of Freudian psychoanalysis or client-centred psychotherapy – yet his doctrine of justification by faith may have something to say to this very issue. This doctrine suggests that true human worth lies not in any ability or quality we may or may not possess, but it lies in the simple fact that we are loved by our creator. At the Heidelberg Disputation of 1518, Luther claimed that: 'Sinners are attractive because they are loved, they are not loved because they are attractive.' He used to say that our righteousness (we might translate this as 'value' or 'worth') lies not *intra nos* (inside us), but *extra nos* (outside us) – in Christ himself. The righteousness of Christians, in which they stand before God, is not their own righteousness, but is Christ's own righteousness, received by faith. They can know that their true value is found not in any good quality in themselves, nor any good actions they might or might not have performed, but in the fact that they are loved by God. This is perhaps the significance for today of Luther's refusal to allow any human contribution to salvation in his stand against Erasmus over the bondage of the will in 1525.

If salvation is dependent upon anything of our own, whether a personal choice or a personal quality, then it comes into doubt. What if we did not make that choice with the right motives? What if we do not live up to the standards set for us? Luther's location of value entirely 'outside ourselves', in God's love manifested in Christ, safeguards a sense that our worth is unshakeable. Whether in work or unemployed, able-bodied or disabled, from an ethnic majority or minority, our worth remains exactly the same. Even if we experience doubt over our own self-worth through despair at our own capabilities, virtue or reputation, this sense of ultimate value cannot be taken away and can become the foundation of a secure and steady self-image.

Beyond this, the doctrine reverses the way in which we tend to evaluate other people. If a person's value lies in a quality or feature which they possess, such as a particular skill or ability or racial characteristics, then it becomes possible to make distinctions between them on those grounds. Some people are more valuable and some are less. An extreme version of this was found in Nazi Germany, where a person's value was located in their loyalty to the party, or their Aryan origins. If, however, as justification by faith insists, a person's true value lies not in anything they possess but in something 'outside themselves' – the fact that they are addressed and loved by God – then we cannot make such distinctions. Each person has dignity and value, and deserves equal treatment, regardless of age, skills, social utility or earning capacity.

There is, however, at the same time a sobering honesty about Luther's doctrine of justification. He insists that the first step to wisdom, or to a rock-solid, immovable sense of self-worth, is to take a good look into the depths of a person's own soul. It means to face up honestly to the self-centredness, lack of love for one's neighbour, cowardice and indifference towards those who are suffering that lurks there. This is no easy doctrine which glosses over the reality of sin and evil in the human heart, the capacity to inflict pain and injustice which lies in everyone.

For Luther, God has to help us to look into this abyss before we can go any further. This is far from that pleasant middle-class religion which assumes that everyone is good and nice, and which refuses to look beneath the surface. Luther's God insists on facing up to the dark secrets inside, the selfish motivations and hidden desires.

But Luther's point is that this is only preliminary. Some forms of religion (both Catholic and Protestant) have implied that this is the sum of religion – making us feel bad about ourselves. Luther insists that if this is in some sense necessary as a first step, it is God's *alien* work, not his *proper* work – it is a means to an end, not an end in itself: 'He makes a person a sinner, so that he may make him righteous.' God breaks up the fragile foundations of a sense of self-worth based in our own virtues, in order to establish a much firmer rock upon which to build. Luther would have been very wary of psychological techniques which try to build self-worth by positive thinking or self-assertion. Faced with real despair, self-doubt and evil, such techniques quickly crumble.

Justification by faith is a reminder to Christians that they approach God not on the basis of who they are, but on the basis of who Christ is. Self-worth, value and forgiveness come as gifts, not as rights. It is nothing to do with achieving the elusive goal of becoming the idealized person they might like to be in their most hopeful moments. It is a reminder that it is only when they stop trying to be someone else, and start being honest about who they really are, that they can begin to receive God's acceptance of them. And only then can they begin to be rebuilt, from within, into people with a solid sense of self-worth, free to give themselves in love and service to their neighbours, freed from the sapping anxiety of self-doubt. It is a reminder that a healthy relationship with God, like any other relationship, can be based only upon one simple thing – trust. It was for that reason that Luther wanted to defend it to the end: 'Whoever touches faith touches the apple of my eye.'

Theology and experience

Theology can often appear from the outside to be dull and irrelevant – barren theory which bears no relation to real life. Luther reminds us of the importance of experience for theology. As he puts it: 'Experience is needed to understand the works of God'. We cannot understand God just by reading books, or by listening to lectures or sermons. Without the experience of being humbled, facing suffering, being tempted, we are like 'donkeys listening to a lyre', unable to make any sense of what we hear.

We have seen how, for Luther, the key test of any theology is suffering. Good theology can help you to stand in the face of temptation, suffering and death; bad theology cannot. From his time as a student, through the monastery and the rediscovery of the gospel, on to the indulgence controversy and further debates with radicals, Luther experienced periods of great distress of heart and soul. Was he saved or damned? Could he be right and all Christendom wrong? How could he love God? The need to face and cope with these experiences of deep despair and paralysing anxiety drove him to find firm ground on which he could stand when the storms were raging. This was, for Luther, the central question – could he find a good and gracious God? In Luther's gospel of God's justification of sinners by grace, received by faith, he found something which answered that question. With this, he could stand on the unshakeable rock of God's solemn word and promise of the forgiveness of sins to those who believe. In this word, which came to him repeatedly in preaching and in the sacraments, God gave the gift of Christ not to the godly, but to the ungodly. Here was solid ground, and he was determined not to shift onto any other ground at all, otherwise he knew that when the storm broke, the foundations would fail.

Hence Luther wants to insist that it is suffering that teaches true theology. The true test of theology is despair. Can it stand when everything else collapses around us? A theology which looks fine and feels good, yet is useless in times of deep distress, is precisely that – useless. This was a theology of fire, a theology tested in suffering and pain. This was the test he wanted to apply to the Zwickau prophets and, in fact, to most of his opponents: 'O that… Erasmus and the sacramentarians could experience the anguish of my heart for only a quarter of an hour!' he wrote to Justus Jonas during the Wittenberg plague in 1527. The message of Christ's righteousness, offered as a gift to the ungodly to be received by faith, only becomes intelligible to those who know only too well that they are ungodly. Those who are secure, self-confident and settled in their own righteousness, and who have never experienced despair or self-doubt, cannot make sense of such a gift.

> 'The love of God does not find, but creates that which is pleasing to it. The love of man comes into being through that which is pleasing to it.'
>
> **Martin Luther at the Heidelberg Disputation, 1518**

Luther's is a theology which makes most sense from a position of failure and struggle. The characteristic temptation of religious people, according to Luther, is to build a 'theology of glory' – in other words, to build a picture of God which accords with what we think he should be like: good, perfect, virtuous, wise and powerful. We then tend to think that God likes only those who are good, perfect, virtuous, wise and powerful, and that he does not like those who are weak, struggling, failing and guilty. We think that the road to God lies through trying to be more virtuous, wise and powerful, and we run away from things such as suffering, pain and failure. Yet these very things are the beginning of true wisdom and virtue.

> 'Only the experience of anguish gives understanding to the hearer, so that the Word of God becomes intelligible to the hearer.'
>
> **Martin Luther, *Operationes in Psalmos*, 1519–21**

So, although he taught in a university, Luther calls into question the notion of purely 'academic theology'. God's word cannot be understood outside of the experience of living the Christian life, with all its uncertainties, doubts and struggles. While theology calls for the highest rigour of thought and serious discipline of mind, it is no merely 'academic' pursuit. It is there to help people to live a good, secure and fruitful life, to enable acts of love to come from the heart, not a guilty conscience. It is there to help people to experience the grace and love of God, and to know God as the good and generous giver which the scriptures present, a God who can be trusted. God is on our side, even though very often it does not feel like it. This is a knowledge which Luther believed could transform people, as it had transformed him: 'Faith must spring up and flow from the blood and wounds and death of Christ. If you see in these that God is so kindly disposed towards you that he even gives his own Son for you, then your heart must grow sweet and disposed towards God. And in this way, your confidence must grow out of pure good will and love – God's towards you and yours towards God.'

'Luther's aim was a spiritual renewal of the church on the basis of intense preoccupation with crucial biblical statements. This renewal would then help theology to perform its real task once more.'

Bernhard Lohse, *Martin Luther's Theology*, 1999

Chronology

10 November 1483: Luther born in Eisleben.

1484–96: Luther's early years and schooling in Mansfeld.

1497: Luther attends school in Magdeburg.

1497–1501: Luther attends Latin school at Eisenach.

1501: Luther's matriculation at Erfurt University.

17 July 1505: Luther enters the Augustinian friary at Erfurt.

1507: Luther ordained priest.

1510–11: Luther's visit to Rome.

1511: Luther's final transfer to Wittenberg University.

1512: Luther awarded doctorate in theology; becomes Professor of Biblical Theology.

1513–15: Luther's first set of lectures on Psalms (*Dictata super Psalterium*).

1515–16: Luther lectures on Romans and Galatians.

September 1517: *Disputation Against Scholastic Theology.*

31 October 1517: *95 Theses on Indulgences.*

April 1518: Heidelberg Disputation.

1518: Melanchthon arrives in Wittenberg.

October 1518: Diet of Augsburg – questioning by Cajetan.

1519: Maximilian I dies – Charles V is elected emperor.

July 1519: Leipzig Disputation, with Karlstadt, against Eck.

June 1520: Papal bull *Exsurge Domine* threatening excommunication issued.

October–November 1520: Three Reformation treatises published.

10 December 1520: Luther burns the papal bull at Wittenberg.

3 January 1521: Luther excommunicated by Pope Leo X.

April 1521: Luther questioned at the Diet of Worms before Emperor Charles V.

December 1521: Zwickau prophets arrive in Wittenberg.

1521–22: Luther in hiding in the Wartburg Castle.

March 1522: Luther returns to Wittenberg; 'Invocavit Sermons'.

1524: Luther's German New Testament published.

October 1524: Luther abandons monastic clothes.

1525: *Twelve Articles of the Peasants* published.

15 May 1525: Battle of Frankenhausen – crushing of peasants' revolt.

13 June 1525: Luther's marriage to Katharine von Bora.

November/December 1525: Luther writes *On the Bondage of the Will* against Erasmus.

1527: Luther experiences severe sickness and depression.

1529: Second Diet of Speyer elicits 'Protest' from evangelical princes.

1–4 October 1529: Marburg Colloquy on the theology of the eucharist.

April–June 1530: Diet of Augsburg – Luther at Coburg Castle.

1534: Publication of the complete German Bible.

1536: *Wittenberg Concord* with the Swiss.

1539: Bigamy of Philip of Hesse.

1543: Luther's attack on the Jews.

1545: Roman Catholic Council of Trent opens.

18 February 1546: Luther's death at Eisleben; funeral in Wittenberg.

Suggestions for Further Reading

There is a vast number of books about Luther and the Reformation. For those who want to read further, here are some which will help fill in the background and take the reader further into Luther's life and thought.

The best and fullest edition of Luther's works in English is the so-called 'American Edition', usually referred to with the initials LW:

J. Pelikan and H. Lehmann, *Luther's Works* (55 volumes), St Louis/Philadelphia: Fortress Press, 1956–75.

Another useful selection is:

T.F. Lull, *Martin Luther's Basic Theological Writings*, Minneapolis: Fortress Press, 1989.

For an account of Luther's theology, look at:

G. Ebeling, *Luther: An Introduction to his Thought*, London: Collins, 1972.

B. Lohse, *Martin Luther's Theology: Its Historical and Systematic Development*, Minneapolis: Fortress Press, 1999.

The fullest biography of Luther in English is Martin Brecht's three-volume account:

M. Brecht, *Martin Luther: His Road to Reformation 1483–1521*, Philadelphia: Fortress, 1985.

M. Brecht, *Martin Luther: Shaping and Defining the Reformation 1521–32*, Minneapolis: Fortress Press, 1990.

M. Brecht, *Martin Luther: The Preservation of the Church 1532–46*, Minneapolis: Fortress Press, 1999.

Other biographies include the following:

R.H. Bainton, *Here I Stand: A Life of Martin Luther*, New York: Abingdon Press, 1950.

H.A. Oberman, *Luther: Man Between God and the Devil*, New Haven: Yale University Press, 1989.

J.M. Todd, *Luther: A Life*, London: Hamish Hamilton, 1982.

More general books on the Reformation:

E. Cameron, *The European Reformation*, Oxford: Clarendon, 1991.

C. Lindberg, *The European Reformations*, Oxford: Blackwell, 1996.

A.E. McGrath, *Reformation Thought: An Introduction*, Oxford: Blackwell, 1999.

S. Ozment, *Protestants: The Birth of a Revolution*, London: Fontana, 1992.

For a taste of some writing from the time:

D.R. Janz (ed.), *A Reformation Reader*, Minneapolis: Fortress Press, 1999.

C. Lindberg, *The European Reformations Sourcebook*, Oxford, Blackwell, 2000.

Index

Other titles from Lion

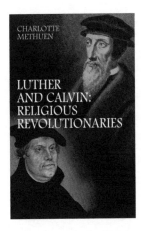

Luther and Calvin: Religious Revolutionaries
Charlotte Methuen

9780745953403

A clear, concise consideration of the context, roles, and messages of these key figures in the Reformation of the 16th century, and how these reformers have shaped the Western world. Perfect for those who want to understand and engage with the ideas and beliefs held by Luther and Calvin.

Charlotte Metheun teaches Church History at the University of Glasgow, and has also worked at the Universities of Hamburg, Bochum, Oxford and Mainz. She is the author of numerous books and articles.

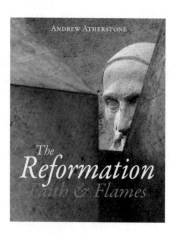

The Reformation
Faith and Flames
Andrew Atherstone

9780745953052

The Reformation marked a period of profound upheaval, possibly the greatest since Christianity was founded in the first century AD. This fully colour illustrated book brings the period to vivid life, looking at why the Reformation happened, how it happened, what it actually was, and what it achieved.

Andrew Atherstone is Tutor in History and Doctrine, and Latimer Research Fellow, at Wycliffe Hall, Oxford. His main research explores aspects of Protestant and Evangelical history.

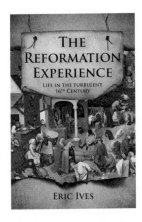

The Reformation Experience
Life in the turbulent 16th century
Eric Ives

9780745952772

There are many sound histories of the Reformation in the old style with its preference for ideas and theologians. Professor Eric Ives' book takes a new approach and shows how the Reformation came to the individual Christian and what it meant. Ives analyses whether (and why) Reformation teaching was accepted or not, and looks at how it changed lives – with particular reference to the parish church, belief, and commitment.

Professor Eric Ives is Emeritus Professor of English History at Birmingham University and is author of the highly acclaimed biography, *The Life and Death of Anne Boleyn*.

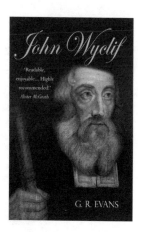

John Wyclif
G.R. Evans

9780745952918

The name of John Wyclif is surrounded by mythology.
The ideas associated with his name had a huge influence
and their effects were felt in the sequence of events
which eventually led to the Reformation.

This major biography offers fresh insights into Wyclif
the man, his preoccupations, and his achievements.
The author follows Wyclif through his childhood and
university days at Oxford to his life as a writer, preacher,
lecturer, and – in his later years – a campaigner against
the abuse of power and privilege. She looks at what
other people have said about Wyclif, his exile in his
parish, and the significant contributions he made
towards the publication of the Bible in English and the
road to Reformation.

G.R. Evans is Professor of Medieval Theology and
Intellectual History at the University of Cambridge. Her
books include works on Anselm, Augustine, Gregory the
Great, and Bernard of Clairvaux, as well as on the study
of the Bible in the Middle Ages.